SOLD:

Marks of a True Disciple

By:

Jared M Price

Scripture quotations are from the ESV® Bible
(The Holy Bible, English Standard Version®)
Copyright © 2001 by Crossway, a publishing
ministry of Good News Publishers.
Used by permission.
All rights reserved.

Acknowledgments:

This book has been over five years in the making. First and foremost, I am ever indebted to my gracious and wise wife Janelle for being both my editor and biggest encourager. Her continual patience, encouragement, and love while writing this book provided me with the time and motivation to finish it. SOLD principles have directly come from our conversations, time in study, and life walking in the military and as parents together. She is my best friend, and I couldn't have finished without her.

My family has been faithful supplementary editors and critics to help me clarify what is in my heart concerning discipleship. I am blessed to have wonderful parents, Jeff and Patti Price, who sacrificed daily to help me know, believe, and follow Jesus Christ. Thank you, Dad and Mom, for showing me the love of God in how you loved me. Thank you for continuing to demonstrate godly living for my family and me. And thank you for your continual encouragement and support in writing this book. Thank you to all my siblings, both blood and by marriage; I greatly appreciate your support and encouragement!

A special thank you to my brother Nathan for his consistent support in developing SOLD and its contents. Nathan and I have taught through SOLD together. His valuable insights and contributions are now included in the updated versions of this book. Thank you for your inspiration, support, and consistent motivation throughout this entire arduous process!

I am also indebted to my in-laws, Steve and Beth Coffey, for their frequent guidance and godly example. Their hearts beat for Jesus, which is reflected in their passion for discipling the unreached. Their sacrificial and joy-filled life is infectious to all those blessed to spend time with them.

A huge thank you to Pastors Kirk Welch and Joe Penberthy from my time at Cornerstone Bible Church. During this season of ministry, I was allotted resources to study discipleship and converse openly with these men on the topic. Additionally, to my close friend and ministry partner,

Caleb Quick, thank you for your encouragement, support, and helpful comments on the final draft.

To all who have been foundational to the contents of this book, my sincere thank you! I hope I have honored the context of all our conversations and study in the fruition of these pages.

With humble thanks,

Jared Michael Price

SOLD: Marks of a True Disciple

SOLD: Marks of a True Disciple

CONTENTS

Introduction:

I was wet, cold, and sandy. I stood in a group of eight young men between 21 and 27. I only knew their last names because it was stenciled on the back and front of their white cotton t-shirts. We all stood facing the instructors, shifting nervously in the soft sand. The historic Naval Amphibious Base on Coronado has one of the most picturesque beaches in the world that few Navy men ever enjoy. During this selection process, the instructors evaluated our individual and team performance to assess our abilities to operate in a highly demanding occupation. As the lead instructor spoke, he had a large object covered by a thick green-colored material behind him.

"Your next evolution is timed. As always, you are being evaluated and graded." Said an average height and build instructor whose eyes were concealed behind thick black lensed glasses. All the instructors wore blacked-out glasses even though it was a rare cloudy southern California day.

My officer selection course held a broad spectrum of activities. Some events were designed to test physical stamina, while others prodded the mind. This specific evolution was the latter. As the instructor explained the rules, several others behind him opened the green bundle and started shuffling through large poles, more thick green material, and rope. Our task was relatively simple. Set up a standard platoon size army tent in less than 30 minutes. With only a few instructions, he started his watch hanging on the clipboard and said, "bust 'em."

Everyone in my group was competing against each other for an officer position. However, this evolution required us to work together to complete a task. Guys naturally began to jockey for leadership roles by speaking the loudest or assuming command of the structural design. Yet, none of us had ever set up a military tent before, let alone one that looked like it hadn't been used since Vietnam. We were not provided any instructions on building the tent other than several guiding principles. Within 10 minutes, it was clear something was wrong. We had the tent skeleton built, and almost all of the equipment was put up, but it looked off. There were two places for two large center poles in the large green cover that would push the ceiling up high, allowing people to walk around easily while providing rigidity to the structure. But we could only find one of these large center poles. My group quickly completed everything we could except for this elusive missing pole. One of the guys looked over to the instructors; we had 9 minutes left. Our group began standing around, not sure of what to do next.

"Are you done?" One of the other instructors asked with a sarcastic grin. The other observers began to laugh and shout condescending remarks. The instructor, whose retinas were still concealed behind his blacked-out glasses, started to ominously write things down on his clipboard.

It was then that it hit me. This was the point of the evolution. That center tent pole was purposely removed. The instructors were testing something. What would we do when we didn't have all the pieces? Would we give up? Would we say good enough? Would we fight amongst ourselves? Or would we continue striving as long as we could to finish the job?

My experience with discipleship was like my selection group trying to put up the tent with one missing pole. I always felt like I was missing something. Questions about discipling, disciple, discipleship, and naught were baffling to me as a young Christian just starting to take my faith seriously. I had enough of a struggle knowing who Paul and Timothy were, let alone finding or making their clone. In my tiny mind, I had no chamber to hold an idea of what discipleship meant or what I was supposed to do to disciple someone else. The material and structure were there. The bible, prayer, and doing "good" things. But I just felt like something was missing. All I knew was that I was told to do something and that something revolved around the word disciple and people. It felt like I was trying to set up a tent with a missing pole.

Dr. Wilkins summarizes the discipleship situation in the following manner at the beginning of his formidable work, *Following the Master.* He says;

> "In the last twenty-plus years, a virtual flood of discipleship studies has swept over the church, yet people may be more confused now than ever. The reason? No consensus reigns in understanding what Jesus was doing and in what we should be doing in making disciples. What is a disciple of Jesus? What should we be like as disciples?"[i]

Dr. Wilkins wrote those words in 1992, and his biblical theology on discipleship is as relevant, if not more so, today as it was then. Although more people are talking about discipleship now, a consensus is still lacking. All the right pieces are not yet evidently in view.

Your experience might be a little different. Maybe you think you were given all the poles. Perhaps you had all the pieces with someone to hold your hand while you tried to create yourself into a "disciple." Perhaps your church had a "discipleship class." You bought a book. Signed up on a white sheet of paper with cold ink to be "discipled." Maybe you were given materials like a workbook with specific questions to work through with someone else. My guess is that you may not have met that person before you signed up. And all of a sudden, you are in a system that is "reproducible," and you are meant to grab someone else and work through that same system with them.

Maybe you are the church pastor, elder, deacon, or small group leader that has had to facilitate a "D-Group" (Discipleship Group). You have likely had a point of frustration, wondering if your efforts were successful. If you had this experience, you might have found your joy depleted and wondering if you were doing things right or not. Your experience may even have brought hopelessness and despair, resulting in questioning your call into ministry.

Today, the church seems to either be giving too little or too much instruction and method in discipleship. One leaves people frustrated, while the other leaves people joyless and paralyzed. The positive in this discussion is that ample discipleship resources are available on discipleship, making disciples, and defining what a disciple is. The church recognizes that while the buildings might be full, people are not becoming disciples of Jesus Christ.

Artificial Christianity is rightly accredited to a lack of true disciples in our congregations. I do not doubt that the Holy Spirit is stirring leaders to put us back on the right track of unity and depth in the body of Christ. With the numerous books, papers, and even national conferences popping up all over, the abundance of voices, however unintentionally, has muddied the waters surrounding the definition of discipleship. My hope is not to be just another voice.

Let me explain what makes this book different than the rest.

What makes this book different?

Unlike many books on being a disciple or disciple making, S.O.L.D. is not primarily a how-to book. This isn't the four-letter acronym that will change your family, ministry team or church in four years. Nor am I pretending to be Yoda and teach how to use the unseen mystical force of these four letters. Instead, I hope that this book serves as a tool to analyze your life through the biblical lens of discipleship. In short:

This book seeks to draw out the Bible's teaching on the marks of a true disciple.

If you claim to be a disciple of Jesus, let me ask one question, is there proof? Apart from the outliers (thief on the cross), Jesus says there will be four proofs of your genuine discipleship. This book walks through these four proofs of discipleship found in four specific teachings of Jesus. Each section of scripture is indicative of a significant redemptive theme. The statements we will look at are the only four places where Jesus defines *the marks of a true disciple.*

The core of this book is the definition of a disciple. I believe that a significant portion of discipleship-related materials has detrimentally missed the definition of a disciple. Christian resources are abundant, with excellent books focusing on methods and strategies of discipleship. Randy Pope wrote the book *InSourcing,* where you will find excellent practical material.[ii] Pope's model of Journey groups and his TEAMS acronym are helpful and easily reproducible. Randy's model offers a biblically-centered practical approach to move passive church members toward active servants of Christ. In Journey Groups, people from all walks of the faith live active gospel relational lives with each other. If you read through *InSourcing,* the book seeks to biblically and practically fulfill the preacher's task from Ephesians 4:11-13. Namely, equipping the saints for the work of ministry. I have no issue with this and am thankful for Pope's work to help the church.

You might have picked up Jim Putman's book *Real-life Discipleship* and found equally helpful material.[iii] Putman defines a disciple as a person whose head, heart, and hands are affected by Christ. This standard definition is obliging and true. Jesus isn't satisfied with part of us but demands all of us. Putman, in his book, develops a discipleship wheel with five stages. In each stage, he seeks to show how a person moves from unbelief to the role of spiritual parent. This wheel provides a fantastic visual and tangible guide for leaders and learners to move people toward spiritual maturity. Like Pope, I believe Putman has practical material that can be incorporated into different church settings for the glory and praise of God.

Also, both books help battle the identified problems of either too little information and no direction or too much information and absolute paralysis. But another central problem emerges. A problem that must be addressed.

A Problem of Definitions

The problem with both authors is not their insightful models to aid people in a closer intimate relationship with God. Nor is the problem in the reproducibility of these models. Both are good.

The problem with them, and I am sad to say with many others, is the misty understanding of *the marks of a true disciple*. Too many authors, bloggers, tweeters, and posters affirm a false dichotomy that being a disciple is somehow different than being a Christian. The two are not separate but mutually inclusive. A disciple must be a Christian, and a Christian must be a disciple.

There is no separation of these identities for Jesus and the New Testament church. And to try and separate them is to build a potentially hazardous and harmful ministry. Suppose someone believes or is affirmed that there is salvation outside of being a true disciple of Jesus. In that case, they are deceived and are living with false hope.

Therefore, the purpose of this book is to present *the marks of a true disciple*. I will do my best not to frustrate you with little direction nor present such a plethora of information you become paralyzed in constant nervous analysis. Rather, I hope that through encountering God's word, you will be encouraged and convicted as you analyze your life through the non-negotiable statements of Jesus on what defines a true disciple.

This book will examine the New Testament's definition of a true disciple throughout the coming pages. True discipleship is identifiable. True discipleship is to a degree measurable. And by the grace of God, true discipleship is attainable. Jesus has made four clear statements describing the marks every true disciple will display. The conclusion from his words is simple.

A true disciple will be S.O.L.D. out for Jesus.

Chapter 1: Definition of Disciple

"Confusion of goals and perfection of means seems, in my opinion, to characterize our age." - Albert Einstein

Growing up in the Pacific Northwest had terrific perks. Unlike the common misconception, there are times when the sun shines in the beautiful state of Washington. I grew up swimming, skiing, mountaineering, wakeboarding, kayaking, and all other sorts of outdoor activities. I loved visiting my grandpa who lived in a beautiful house on Lake Joy as a kid.

The lake is rather small for Washington lakes. In the summers, my friends and I would swim out to a high dive platform in the middle and have various sorts of competitions. Besides flawlessly executing a can opener off the high dive, my favorite thing about Lake Joy was the morning. If you wake up before sunrise, there is a mystic layer of fog covering the lake's top. I loved pulling up a chair and reading my Bible amidst the sounds of woodpeckers and reflections of evergreens. The lake looks like a mirror in the morning, perfectly frozen except for the occasional ripples caused by a bass catching its morning fly for breakfast.

My grandpa had moved all the stones from the shoreline to a neatly lined pile near the dock. Whenever the lake was at its finest reflection, I would toss a stone in to break it up. I don't know why I did it. Perhaps, it was just teenage destruction syndrome. But watching one stone enter the motionless reflection of fog and evergreens was enchanting. I could see every perfect ripple as they extended further and further out into the lake. Occasionally, I would grab an entire handful and throw them all in at once. What was the result? Chaos. Identifying a specific ripple from an individual stone is next to impossible.

I believe the same is true concerning the definition of a disciple. With so many voices splashing, with their ever so slightly different perspectives, it is hard to come back to the source of the individual ripples. But that is exactly what is needed to cure the chaos. It is essential to come back to the source and recover the nature of a disciple.

Again, by no means are people intentionally trying to create a definition pond of chaos. However, that is a byproduct of multiple interpretations and modern contextualization. Discipleship has several vantage points from which we can observe it. As a result, when an individual or group desires to expand upon one vantage point, the unintended outcome is a loss of the other views.

Think about how you put together a puzzle. For me, tunnel vision sets in and it is easy to get caught up trying to put together one section of the puzzle. But in the frantic disorder of trying to complete one section, a piece or two might accidentally get shoved off the table. And now, just like the tent in my officer selection group, you are left without the full picture.

This chapter hopes to put all the pieces on the table and assemble the whole picture. And we shall see it is a humbling and terrifying reality when the full picture of discipleship is assembled.

Identifying the Pieces

Dictionary Definition

The first picture of the puzzle is the dictionary definition.

Let's begin by making sure we are clear on the definition of disciple. We receive the word disciple from the Greek word μαθητής (mathētēs). The plainest sense of this word is a follower, or the infinitive, to follow. The biblical linguists Louw and Nida, define this as "to acquire information as the result of instruction, whether in an informal or formal context."[iv] Being a disciple revolves around the flow of knowledge and understanding.

People today use different words to convey the same meaning. When you listen to an artist talk about their idols of inspiration or a writer refer to their literary heroes, they are speaking in discipleship terms. The major difference between today and the Greco-Roman world is that the information age has allotted us to follow everyone.

Depending on what source you ask, the average Instagram user has 213 followers. I am sure that in writing that number, it will change by the time you read it! Between all the social media platforms, anyone can "follow" thousands of people at once. Discipleship today is as common of a practice as it was in biblical times; it just looks different. Instead of daily spending 4-8 hours learning and inquiring from one person, we spend 1-2 minutes with 213 people. Additionally, discipleship has morphed from an interactive relationship to pure individual reception. In a social media generation, followers often have no personal or virtual interaction with their disciplers other than the occasional "like" or "comment" on a post.

Make no mistake, discipleship is as common today as in the ancient world. It just appears dissimilar. To properly understand discipleship, we must examine its original historical context, the next section of the puzzle.

Historical Context

If we investigate the early Greco-Roman world, we can see the inner workings of the scholarly disciple. When Alexander the Great conquered the known Mediterranean world, Greece spread Hellenistic culture to all the regions. The common trade language became Greek, and as a result, customs, education, philosophy, and other practices spread throughout the lands. Within this Hellenistic context, these scholarly disciples, or students, were known as followers or pupils.[v] Students were primary academic learners who obligated themselves to a specific knowledgeable master. Much like our universities and their specific schools or academic majors today.

Strong parallels with the biblical idea of a disciple exist within this definition. The disciples often refer to Jesus as their teacher, as in Mark 4:38, when they fear perishing. Jesus himself uses this classical definition in Matthew 10:24 to refer to how a teacher is above his disciples. Most importantly, in the great commission in Matthew 28:20, Jesus instructs them to *teach* all that he has commanded. Clearly, scripture's perspective of discipleship includes intentional instruction.

Yet, there are examples of this scholarly brand of disciple in ancient Greece that end up improving, or I might say emerging, from their master's teachings after their death. While there are significant examples, the most prevailing is Socrates.

Wilkins identifies how Pythagoras and the Sophists were the first to use the term. Socrates immediately rejected the term disciple because of its affiliation with Sophist philosophy, only to later accept its use in terms of relationship. Wilkins notes that for Socrates, "becoming a disciple of a particular culture meant that one's lifestyle now reflected that culture."[vi] When Aristotle became Socrates' disciple, it was about the relationship between master and student and adapting to Socrates' lifestyle. At least while he was alive.

Aristotle studied intently under Socrates. He adopted his methods, beliefs, and even his manner of rhetoric. However, after Socrates' death, Aristotle changed from his master's teaching.

Aristotle had been taught to see enlightenment and knowledge in the spiritual or supernatural world. Once free of Socrates' oversight, Aristotle's perspective shifted. He saw the value and worth in understanding the physical realm. He ended up believing true knowledge and enlightenment came from studying and pondering the material things of this world rather than the immaterial.

This outlook reversal was not uncommon between disciples and their teachers. Improving upon, changing, and correcting a previous master's teaching after their death was accepted as a continual quest for knowledge.

Scientifically, correction and improvement upon previous thoughts or ideas should be praised. If people simply accept what was said as truth, we will lack progress and growth as humanity. Atheists and agnostics often criticize Christians for embracing primitive beliefs held by inferior teachers. In their eyes, we have moved past such beliefs as Aristotle moved past Socrates. That isn't to say we disregard them as people; we simply have found a more enlightened truth to adhere to.

Naturally, this is problematic when we consider objective truths. To reject Jesus' words, or to improve upon them, is to reject Jesus himself. Jesus said clearly, "the one who rejects me and does not receive my words has a judge; the word that I have spoken will judge him on the last day" (John 12:48).

Therefore, the historical definition of disciple changes with Jesus. No disciple attempts to add to or change his words. They embrace them. Listen to Paul in Colossians 2:6-7, "Therefore, as you received Christ Jesus the Lord, so walk in him, rooted and built up in him and established in the faith, just *as you were taught,* abounding in thanksgiving." The type of instruction a disciple of Jesus offers is identical to the teaching they received from Jesus. Just as 1 Corinthians 11:1 says, "Be imitators of me, as I am of Christ."

The instruction doesn't change, although the relationship might. As the early church progresses and grows, the teaching continues to be about Jesus. Improvement, modification, or "what Jesus really said" scenarios are non-existent or quickly rejected as false.

With this in mind, two truths about the biblical definition puzzle become clear. One, discipleship involves the intentional communication of information between two parties. Two, instruction happens relationally while the subject of instruction is rooted in a singular context, God's word.

Biblical Context

Let's put together another section in the puzzle: The New Testament's use of the word. In the New Testament, there are various kinds of disciples mentioned. There are the classic disciples in the relationship between Aristotle and Socrates. These disciples would pay great sums of money to learn under respected teachers. Then there are Rabbinic disciples, as was common in the day, which John the Baptist, Jesus, and the Pharisees had (Matt. 9:14, Mark 2:18, Luke 5:33).

Rabbinic disciples were chosen or selected to follow and learn from a specific Rabbi from a young age. Paul, for example, studied under the revered Rabbi Gamaliel (Acts 22:3). Disciple's eventually replaced their rabbis and took over their responsibilities in the community. It was a great honor to be a disciple, and although it often involved giving up precious years, it was worth the price. This further supports the relational aspect of discipleship.

Another way the term was used was to associate with a specific person's teachings. In John 9:28 the Pharisees are accusing the man born blind of being a disciple of Jesus, while they declare themselves disciples of Moses. Wilkins defines this "discipleship [as] a personal commitment to a type of teaching as represented in a person who is known to speak for God."[vii] This form of discipleship was common during the early Greco-Roman era as the historical scholastic use was adopted into religious circles.

The gospels reveal the twelve disciples had very normal discipleship expectations. Jesus' disciples are expected to learn, follow, perform tasks, and teach others the teachings of their master. And at the end, the disciples are given their master's work after his death. As Wilkins notes, what we see in the early Jewish context is that "Jesus' disciples did not seem to be much different from other types of disciples who surrounded other masters in Israel."[viii] Everything we have discussed so far appears to be culturally consistent and normal within the historical and biblical contextual use of the word *disciple.*

Not Yet Complete

At this point, many authors and pastors think the picture is complete, the tent is finished, and all the pieces are in place. The term disciple is now solidified. Disciple simply means an intentional relationship between a teacher and a student for intellectual instruction. To be a disciple is to be a life learner of another person. Some authors want to draw similarities between the biblical idea of a disciple to that of a mentor-mentee.

In his book *Growing Up,* Robby Gallaty wants his readers to know that the term mentor is synonymous with someone who disciples. Additionally, to be a mentee is equal to being a disciple. Robby appears from our study to be right. Both secular Greek and the Bible portray the disciple relationship like our contextual mentor-mentee relationship. Logically, this leads Gallaty to urge his readers to engage in life mentorship relationships within their specific local church contexts.

Our cultural definition of mentor seems to work. We view the mentors as typically more advanced in age and life experience. Someone willing to get into our lives and speak wisdom into various situations. In his book, Robby argues for the necessity of these mentor-type relationships in what he calls D-Groups. He claims these mentors to mentee groups are essential in fulfilling the great commission set before us by Jesus.[ix]

Dennis McCallum and Jessica Lowery take this up as well in a slightly different direction. In their book *Organic Discipleship*, the authors claim that "one of the main goals of discipleship is to provide the body of Christ with leaders and role models who can teach others and lead Bible studies, ministry teams, or home groups."[x] McCallum and Lowery see discipleship as creating leaders for the church. Discipleship for these authors solves the church attendee problem. Too many people just want to attend and not get involved. They assert that is why we have discipleship, to help people move to leadership, action, and service.

Another voice is Jonathan K. Dodson. In his book *Gospel Centered Discipleship,* Dodson steps back and analyzes the term through what he calls "gospel glasses."[xi] By analyzing the great commission, he shows that a true disciple is rational, relational, and missional. He summarizes his findings into this succinct definition: "A disciple of Jesus, then, is someone who learns the gospel, relates in the gospel, and communicates the gospel."[xii]

Jonathan seeks to clarify confusion on the target of discipleship. He asks the question, "Is discipleship for maturing believers or is it for evangelizing unbelievers?" Analyzing this question with gospel lenses clears it up. It is neither one nor the other. For Jonathan, it is both.

Robby, Dennis, Jessica, and Jonathan are all hitting on respectable contemporary understandings and implications of discipleship. They all seek to incorporate the word's definition, historical context, and biblical context. And certainly, the church should apply these principles already learned since it was the vessel Jesus used to characterize believers in him.

Unfortunately, the puzzle is not complete; something is missing. While all the sections might have been put together, there are several holes, missing pieces preventing us from seeing the full picture. Perhaps, they have simply been overlooked. But regardless, the puzzle is not complete.

Scripture transforms disciple from what it meant to the Greeks, Romans, and Rabbis to something altogether different. When Jesus changes the understanding of disciple, it becomes a simple and yet complex vessel. The term now includes all those transformed by the power of God from spiritual death to life.

Picking up the Pieces

Scholars debate on whether discipleship is meant to evangelize the lost or mature believers. Jonathan Dodson has helpfully shown this to be an unnecessary and wrong dichotomy. When we peer into the New Testament, the reason why is clear.

The first piece that tends to be missing is simply that there is no division between Christian and disciple in the mind of Jesus or the early church. Wilkins defines the specific biblical definition of disciple as "one who has come to Jesus for eternal life, has claimed Jesus as Savior and God, and has embarked upon the life of following Jesus." With that, the definition of "discipleship" is then the "ongoing process of growth as a disciple."[xiii]

Discipleship then doesn't start before conversion. While a person can be in the process of becoming a disciple as an unbeliever (i.e. disciple making), the term disciple cannot be accurately applied until they surrender and believe in Jesus. A person is a disciple and is being discipled the moment they become a Christian. The term Christian or follower of Christ and disciple are synonymous. They are fused. They are a marriage to which there is no divorce. If a person seeks to be a Christian, they must become a disciple. If a person seeks to become a true disciple, they must become a Christian.

There is confusion in Christianity on discipleship because the Bible uses all three different understandings of the term disciple. The traditional understanding of secular Greek and Rabbi's is seen when referring to Jesus' disciples in the gospels. But then Jesus transforms and changes this term forever. He renovates it into a vessel for identifying those who have truly believed and submitted to his words. The conversion of this term is seen clearly in the New Testament.

The Gospels

First, the Gospels present both the normal Greco-Roman use of disciple, and a new definition in Jesus' teaching. In John's Gospel, the first mention of the term disciple is about John the Baptist. John 1:35-50 describes how Andrew, Peter, Nathanael, and one unnamed follower begin following Jesus. Both Andrew and the unnamed disciple overheard John the Baptist describe Jesus as the Lamb of God and decided to follow him. This is referencing them as a disciple in the common understanding of the term who can detach and reattach themselves to various teachers as they desire and feel so inclined.

At this point, the disciples are functioning in the normal Greco-Roman understanding of this term. They follow a man they believe to be a more extraordinary spiritual leader than John the Baptist. But at the beginning, they think of themselves as no more than learners or pupils of Jesus. Many functioned like this and are called disciples. In Matthew 8:21 a disciple comes to Jesus and asks to bury his father. However, he is met with a shocking reply: he should let the dead bury their own dead.

Mark 2:18 and Luke 5:33 describe how both the Pharisees and John also have disciples. Yet, they both hold to traditional understandings of Judaism, whereas Jesus' disciples follow a new teaching. In these examples, we can see that though there are some differences, the disciples are seen by the rest of the religious community as similar followers and learners of a teacher.

However, Jesus does not correct teachings but demands something new. He requires a kind of follower who completely submits, obeys, and worships him alone. In John 6, Jesus delivers a difficult message. At the end of the message, many of his disciples heard the words he had spoken and said, "This is a hard saying, who can listen to it?" (John 6:60). Six verses later, we see these acclaimed disciples of Jesus desert him.

It is at this juncture where Jesus begins to explain what his requirements are of a true disciple. A true disciple, Jesus said, will abide in his words (John 8:31), they will submit to him over all relationships and relinquish all things for him (Luke 14:25-33), they will love others as Christ has loved them (John 13:34-35), and they will worship and glorify God by bearing fruit (John 15:8). These characteristics identify true disciples, and these true disciples will go forward and make more disciples for Jesus. Already, the term has been transformed by Jesus to refer to a specific tribe or group of people whose whole lives are Jesus'.

Acts

Secondly, in Acts, we see this term take on a new meaning. This time the word disciple is used about true believers of Jesus in a given area, making the word synonymous with church and Christians. Acts 11:26 shows this the best. It says, "For a whole year they met with the church and taught a great many people. And in Antioch, the *disciples* were first called *Christians.*"

In this verse, Paul and Barnabas go to the gathering of believers in Antioch. This is the gathered Church, and the disciples are said to be what makes up the Church. Notice how the text states explicitly that it is at Antioch, where they were first called Christians. This term "Christians" refers to those who gathered as a "Church" or called themselves disciples of Christ. Notice Luke's intentionality to identify a change in the functional terminology used to describe the early church. The terms Christian and disciple appear to be interchangeable.

Throughout Acts, this connection between the terms disciple and Christian are used in tantamount. In Acts 9:1, it says that "Saul was still breathing threats against the disciples of the Lord." "Disciples" are identified as true followers of Christ and are called Christians later in 11:26. There is also a reference to "the Way." Again, this is simply another way to describe the Christian faith. These terms are used in Acts 9:2, 19:9, 23, 24:14, 22, referring to those who follow Jesus Christ. It was called the Way because Christ's disciples believed that the only way to eternal life with God was through his Son, Jesus Christ.

Out of all these terms used to describe the individual and corporate followers of Christ, the two that remain universally accepted today are Christian and Church. But for some reason, we have not retained the traditional title of a disciple for the true believer in Jesus.

Epistles

Lastly, we need to consider the absence of the term disciple in the epistles. Some authors debate why there is no mention of disciple, discipleship, or only one reference to Christian in all the Epistles. While this is true, we need to remember a few things about the epistles in general.

The epistles, by nature, are primarily letters to various churches. Consequently, they often address the believing community and not one disciple, believer, or Christian. And even with the case of Philemon, where there is one recipient, the letter is still meant to be read in the hearing of the church. Therefore, the intended audience of these letters is the corporate body of Jesus Christ. The absence of the word disciple, or only one reference to Christian, shouldn't surprise us. We should expect a more familial language that would work in conjunction with the body of Christ. Thus, we see terms like brother and sister or father and mother being used.

Jesus revolutionizes the idea of being a disciple and gives it a completely new meaning. No longer is a disciple simply a follower and pupil or life-on-life learner. Jesus changes the term to refer to those who surrender entirely to Him as Savior and Lord. No true disciple of Christ ever improves upon his teaching. Disciples of Christ submit to Him. There is only allegiance to Christ and surrender of oneself to be transformed by Him.

This missing piece, namely that Christian and disciple are synonymous, reveals possible hazards if a false dichotomy between Christian and disciple is affirmed.

Implications of an Incomplete Puzzle

The implication of a missing puzzle piece is pure frustration. Naturally, you will look on the floor, move chairs, turn on more lights, and do whatever is necessary to find the missing piece. Why? Because the picture is incomplete. It is not finished. Something is missing. And this missing piece has devastating implications when disciple is defined as anything other than synonymous with Christian.

As mentioned, Gallaty has written practically helpful methods to assist in making disciples but confuses this point. Do not misunderstand my position; Gallaty deals with many positive and incredibly helpful things and does so gracefully. However, there is an implied meaning that being a disciple is somehow different than being a Christian. He gives the following analogy describing all Christians:

> "Every Christian could be compared to one of two bodies of water: the Jordan River, or the Dead Sea. The Jordan River is an active body of water, flowing from north to south. The Dead Sea, on the other hand, has no outlets. Water comes in from the north to the lowest point in the world, and it doesn't flow back out. So the water is stagnant; it just sits there. I believe that every Christian is like one of these bodies of water. You are either flowing as God uses you to impact the lives of other people, or you are dead."[xiv]

Does the Bible lead us to believe that there can be someone who has been purchased by the blood of Jesus Christ, forgiven of their sin, secured with the seal of the Holy Spirit, and promised eternal life with God almighty only to be stagnate and useless like the Dead Sea? That type of person does not fit any of scripture's proofs for sincere conversion. Instead, the Dead Sea description more rightly fits that of a false disciple who has never surrendered themselves to the Lordship of Jesus Christ. There are no Dead Sea Christians, only living conduits for Jesus.

Two terrible possible implications emerge when being a disciple is viewed as an optional means for maturity.

False Confirmation of Salvation

The first tragic outcome is churches become full of unregenerate self-acclaimed Christians. If discipleship is placed post-conversion, then churches will continue to affirm false converts of their professions of faith and wrongly identify unforgiven sinners as saints.

When Jesus addresses the church at Laodicea, his words reveal that faithless false disciples made up that church. In Revelation 3:14-16 he said, "I know your works: you are neither cold nor hot. Would that you were either cold or hot! [16] So, because you are lukewarm, and neither hot nor cold, I will spit you out of my mouth."

Those who read this verse to be a stern rebuke to repentant Christians should consider the rest of the passage. Jesus says in verses 19-20, "those whom I love, I reprove and discipline, so be zealous and repent. [20] Behold, I stand at the door and knock. If anyone hears my voice and opens the door, I will come in to him and eat with him, and he with me." These people call themselves members of the church, yet they are separated from Jesus by their sin. The door of repentance only needs to be opened to receive forgiveness, but they have yet to open the door.

Today churches and evangelistic organizations affirm conversions of people who truly have never heard nor comprehended what it means to be a disciple of Jesus.

On the fourth of July, I worked as a traffic volunteer for the local firework show a few years back. I was able to meet several high school students during the event. I remember one 17-year-old girl, we will call her Bethany, in particular, because of the conversation we had. I asked the whole group if they went to church anywhere around that area, and Bethany replied quickly. She said she had attended the same church since she was a baby and helped lead worship there. Bethany's family helped plant the church, and they were often the first ones there and among the last to leave.

I immediately was excited and thought Bethany, and I could tag team this group of students and get into rich Christ-centered conversations. That is when I put the ball on the tee for Bethany. I asked her to explain the gospel to all these other students. Bethany froze. She wasn't a shy girl by any means, but at this moment, she stood looking at me as if I had asked her an AP Calculus question. After some prodding, it was clear that Bethany neither knew the gospel, nor the reason for Jesus' death, and why we are called to believe in him.

I believe that Bethany had heard these answers week in and out at her church. She had probably sung them repeatedly. In short, Bethany's church had affirmed her presence and participation as genuine faith, but she never surrendered herself as a disciple of Jesus. The church's wrong assumption about a profession of faith led to Bethany's false assurance of salvation and ultimately unregenerate heart.

Church Hierarchy

The second outcome is less disastrous but still damaging. Hierarchy in the church. If discipleship is optional, then it becomes a post-salvation Christian pedestal platform that breeds pride in some and timidity in others. And suppose you are high up on the pedestal. In that case, you can graduate from being just a regular disciple to a disciple maker. That gets you two gold stars, a lollypop, your pastor's pat on the back, and a thumbs up from Jesus. This dichotomy also breeds division amongst the members depending on who discipled them. The confusion and unfaithfulness amongst God's people from this unfortunate misunderstanding are seen in the Church at Corinth during the first century.

The church in Corinth had significant problems. Various sexual sins, people getting drunk off communion, disagreements, factions, and questions regarding foods sacrificed to idols. But the first issue Paul addresses is individual believers in the same Church being divided amongst each other based on who discipled them.

Paul says, "What I mean is that each one of you says, "I follow Paul," or "I follow Apollos," or "I follow Cephas," or "I follow Christ... What then is Apollos? What is Paul? Servants through whom you believed, as the Lord assigned to each" (1 Cor. 1:12; 3:5). Paul boils it down neatly, disciple makers are nothing more than fellow servants of Christ. However, the church in Corinth had put these men in higher categories. The result was their followers accrued arrogance by association. This mentality produced divided and proud individuals who were arrogant from their learning or timid and stagnant because of a lack of it.

Today we see many of these problems arise in churches of all sizes. The Christian war that I have personally been affected by was Mark Driscoll and John MacArthur and their disciples. The tension between these two pastors was extraordinary, resulting in subsequent tension-filled conversations between those who adhered to their teachings. I remember being drilled on my first pastorate interview about my perspective on Mark Driscoll. This interviewer intended to find out why I would listen to a preacher such as Mark Driscoll. Intriguing enough, the teaching I was receiving from Driscoll at that time was identical to what I was being persuaded to listen to from MacArthur.

Though there are multiple intrinsic factors at work, the major problem is people were discipled by men rather than discipled to be like the God-man, Jesus Christ.

A Complete Picture

When the pieces are all put together and the picture is complete, it presents the undeniable marks of a disciple. We cannot explain away Jesus' strong demands as only applicable to a select few, take them allegorically, or rationalize them based on cultural context. Jesus makes four clear, unambiguous, and undeniable statements that summarize what genuine followers of him will demonstrate in their lives. And these statements apply to every aspect of life. The marks of a true disciple provide a lens through which we can examine and measure our faithfulness.

A disciple is a Christian. And a true disciple is someone who will Sacrifice, Obey, Love, and Disciple others for Jesus.

Yes, this is a bold claim. The inference of this definition is clear. Suppose there is no sacrifice, obedience, love, or discipleship of others present in a person's life. In that case, that person is not a Christian.

We will explore this definition throughout this book and look in-depth at its implications. In general, this definition informs our thinking and actions in ecclesiology, family, work, finances, politics, and society.

The full picture informs how we examine and think through the church. Our ecclesiology, what we believe about the church, is directly affected by what we believe about discipleship. If Jesus' demands of his disciples is just for higher tier Christians, you know the really committed people, then we can easily excuse ourselves from his directives by supposing they do not apply to our situation. Additionally, it may lead to a push for a profession of faith rather than committed followers of Christ. Our services, social engagement, missions trips, small groups, children's ministries, and other programs may solely measure the church's success on the number of annual converts. The Church turns from the body of Christ to Christians Incorporated. Every member is a sales representative. Trained and equipped with the best apologetic sales tactics to convince a person to profess belief and enter an organization with benefits that rival Facebook and Google. The full picture of discipleship focuses and steers the church from obtaining an arbitrary number of professions to making S.O.L.D. out disciples for Jesus.

The full picture informs our understanding of marriage. My marriage is not primary for or about me. I remember sitting on the couch at my professor's house as he and his wife conducted my and

Janelle's third pre-marital counseling session. I had just explained in detail why I wanted to marry Janelle. Honestly, I thought I had crushed their question in a romantic but honest fashion and had earned some major points. However, after pausing to analyze my answer, he looked at me. He said, "Essentially, you want to marry Janelle so that she can make your life better." I looked at him with a puzzled expression. Then with grace and kindness, he and his wife exposed how my thoughts about marriage were based on my selfish desires and emotions. They took us through the scriptures and explained how a disciple is called to sacrifice self and serve their spouse like Christ. The definition of disciple allows us to honestly assess our marriages according to our S.O.L.D. out heart for Jesus.

The full picture provides a measurement for Christian parenting. Involvement in the local body of disciples is not optional. Like every other red-blooded sinner, I have thought, "Do I really need to go to church today? They won't even miss me, and besides, I have so many other things to do!" But as we will discover in later chapters when we encounter the demands of Jesus upon his disciples we realize what we often think we need to do, and what Jesus calls us to do, are in opposition to one another. The things we prioritize, plan around, and sacrifice for are normally not the things that Jesus demands of us. Jesus does not care if your child can swing a bat, kick a ball, or ace a test. He cares that they love the Lord their God with all their heart, mind, soul, and strength. Jesus wants their obedience more than the actualization of their gifted talents. The full picture of discipleship helps us trust Jesus with our children's future while being mindful of their presence. With a precise and clear definition, we can measure how we lead our children in becoming S.O.L.D. out for him.

The full picture changes how we approach work. The demands of Jesus are imposing not only on church and family but your professional sphere. Work is not an occupation for a disciple to achieve personal recognition, popularity, accomplishment, fulfillment, or financial prosperity. Work is a blessing so that you can bless others. A disciple's professional occupation is a platform to display the gospel of Jesus Christ. In every aspect, the full picture of discipleship is to radiate in our work and demonstrate a S.O.L.D. out passion for Jesus.

The full picture shifts how we evaluate our disposition to politics. Jesus sets us free from our bondage to sin, but our perspectives on policy are not free to interpretation as a disciple. We surrender freedom to rationalize and justify according to our own presuppositions. There is an objective right and wrong. As will be discussed later, certain aspects of policy are not open debate, but are definitive. A disciple surrenders their feelings freely to Jesus and actively submits to representing his truth in every aspect of life. The full picture of discipleship will push us to uncomfortable and difficult positions. This will be hard to accept for many people because we are called to live S.O.L.D. out for Jesus.

The full picture gives us a way to assess our social habits. There is someone you do not like. Their name likely immediately popped into your head as you are reading this. Socially, we tend to interact and gravitate toward either people we are most similar to or want to be like. But Jesus' call is frequently counter to our natural desire. A disciple is called to love the person we like the least. Genuine discipleship seeks out relationships that provide the disciple with no personal benefit. Our social interaction is not so much about us as it is being S.O.L.D. out for Jesus.

Disciple and Christian are synonymous. Therefore, just as the implications of the Christian faith effect every area of life, so the marks of a disciple stretch into every corner of our lives. Jesus says to come and follow him. He doesn't say that we can follow him how we like, want, or how we think he meant. We are called to follow him in every aspect of our life whether we agree with it or not. Whether we like it or not. Whether we think what he is asking is right or not.

Summary

Even if all the sections are complete, one or two missing pieces can distort a puzzle. Suppose the puzzle of the definition of a disciple is left incomplete. In that case, it will continue to cause catastrophic implications for the church. The church is not in the business of creating motivational speakers, positive life mentors, sensitive, emotional growth groups, or self-help solutions. None of us can provide what every person desperately needs.

Jesus.

The Church exists to make disciples of Jesus Christ. We cannot confuse the definition of this word.

To be a disciple is to be a Christian. And a true disciple will be S.O.L.D. out for Jesus.

When we embrace this reality, it changes our perspective on what Jesus says his disciples will look like. It informs what we think about how we live this life. In the next chapter, investigate with me the words of Jesus on what it means to be a disciple. What we find first is discipleship costs nothing, yet at the same time, it costs everything.

Chapter 2: The Cost of Discipleship

"Discipleship is not an offer that man makes to Christ." - Dietrich Bonhoeffer

Basic Underwater Demolition / SEAL (BUD/S) training is regarded as the most challenging training program in the United States military. Every year, young men from all over the country compete in a selection pool to earn a contract to attempt training. This selection process takes significant time, training, and dedication to complete an application packet that surpasses the other thousands of prospective students. Most train and prepare for years before selection. And of the small percent finally selected to attend training, over eighty percent will fail. Once the chosen few are designated, they will go through the most physically demanding six-month regiment of their life. BUD/S is broken up into three phases. The first phase is where students will undergo the legacy evolution that all SEALs have accomplished—hell week.

Hell week results in the highest attrition of students over the shortest amount of time. Anytime during training, a student has the opportunity to Drop On Request, or DOR. They do this by ringing a bell, which signals to their class and the instructor cadre that they have quit the program. During hell week, the bell follows the class everywhere they go for 5 and ½ days. In the 132 hours of hell week, students have the opportunity to sleep for a maximum of 4 hours, will run over 200 miles, which is 7.5 marathons. Most of that mileage is spent in a six-man boat crew, running with an IBS boat on top of their heads.

In my hell week, the bell began ringing the first hour. It continued ringing until sometime into the afternoon on Wednesday. By Wednesday night, our class was solidified. No one else would quit. The class continued regardless of raw skin, fractured bones, dislocated shoulders, pulmonary edema, hypothermia, or any of the other weird diagnosis' we had. Finishing hell week didn't feel real. Looking back, it felt like one really really really long terrible day, that ended as suddenly as it began. And eventually, after the swelling and pains healed, comfort returned—At least for a time.

People's favorite question is, "why do people quit BUD/S?" I had an officer and friend in my class who came to BUD/S from a few years in the fleet. He was a Naval Academy graduate and an outstanding athlete, in pristine physical shape, and seasoned with life experience. During the first day of first phase, he quit within 10-minutes of breakout. I asked him later on why he rang the bell. I don't remember his exact words, but he said something to this effect:

"In that moment during breakout, I realized what I was going to have to do, and I decided I didn't want to do that."

In the early hours of that Monday morning, my friend counted the cost of BUD/S and realized he didn't want to pay it. In the first few minutes of that dark cold Monday morning—he quit. He quit because he knew he would have to spend the next 6-months getting comfortable being uncomfortable. And BUD/S was just the beginning. He let his mind wander into the unknowns of the job, the demands on the family, and the potential risk of mortality. He concluded he didn't want that life. Regardless of any personal disappointment, I respected that he counted the cost.

As people, we are *driven* recklessly into making various decisions. This includes decisions to join the Navy as much as it includes decisions to follow Christ. People commit to following a

Christ that they may not fully understand. I say *driven* purposefully. Unfortunately, it happens where the evangelizing Christian or emotionally charged church service is to blame for a person's ill-informed and possibly pressured response to Christ.

I speak from my own experience. I have so passionately desired people to be saved and become a disciple of Jesus that I nearly force them into a decision through argument and emotion. But a flippant pressured decision will likely make ringing a bell more appealing than carrying a boat. That is why Jesus sternly charges those who come to him to count the cost.

Count the Cost

Jesus takes an opportunity in Luke 14 to speak to a newly assembled crowd about what it takes to follow Him.

The first thing he says is, "If anyone comes to me and does not hate his own father and mother and wife and children and brothers and sisters, yes, and even his own life, he cannot be my disciple. Whoever does not bear his own cross and come after me cannot be my disciple." This goes against every speech, preaching, or public speaking course I have ever taken. Jesus presents no bait and hook. He states explicitly and unapologetically what he demands—everything.

Jesus gives two illustrations expressing the embarrassment and potentially disastrous outcomes of not counting the cost before beginning an activity. He concludes with verse 33, "So therefore, any one of you who does not renounce all that he has cannot be my disciple." The continued refrain is someone "cannot" be a disciple without loving Jesus above all other relationships and surrendering everything to Him. Jesus demands everything.

Dietrich Bonhoeffer, the famous German pastor, and

theologian, coined the often-quoted phrase, "when Christ calls a man he bids him come and die."[xv] Jesus does not just call pastors, missionaries, or para-church ministers to a life of surrender; he bids every person who claims faith in Him to come and die. Michael Horton concurs and goes further, "God is not a supporting actor in our drama; it is the other way around. God does not exist to make sure that we are happy and fulfilled. Rather, we exist to glorify God and to enjoy him forever."[xvi] When a sinner surrenders to Christ, they abandon all of who they are.

Mark 8:35 says, "For whoever would save his life will lose it, but whoever loses his life for my sake and the gospel's will save it." Being a disciple means complete surrender to Jesus' Lordship.

Now some may ask, what about the other passages like the famous John 3:16 where it says all you need to do is believe? What about the whole burden being light thing? Doesn't Romans 10:9 say we just need to confess with our mouth and believe in our heart? Doesn't Ephesians say we are saved by no work of our own and it is a gift of God? All this talk about absolute surrender, lordship, and personal death sounds a lot like a works-based religion. Didn't Martin Luther divert us from this concept of a works-based religion 500 years ago? How can Jesus say that all we need to do is believe and then flip it around and say we need to renounce all things to follow Him? Since you say being a disciple is synonymous with being a Christian, are you then saying there are conditions to salvation other than faith?

Okay, hold the whole heretic hotline for a second. All I want to do is expose the seeming contradiction in scripture over our discipleship. This is a historic and ongoing discussion on the nature of our salvation. Sadly, the modern context of the discussion is solely in the realm of soteriology (the study of salvation) and is rarely discussed with relevance to discipleship.

The terms Antinomianism and Legalism are helpful terms to categorize these polar opposite perspectives. Mark Jones has written an incredibly insightful book titled *Antinomianism,* covering this discussion in excellent detail. In the most basic sense, Antinomianism stresses belief in Christ to the negation of the law. On the opposite spectrum, legalism holds to conditional salvation based on obedience to the commands of scripture.

Historically, these views have been at each other's throat. However, Jones' research shows an intriguing surprise. Jones cites the work of Oliver O'Donovan when he says "legalism and antinomianism are in fact two sides of the same coin because they are 'fleshly' ways of living life." He then concludes, "The grace of God in the person of Jesus Christ, properly understood, is the only solution to these twin heresies. In essence, the mistakes of legalism and antinomianism are Christological errors."[xvii]

Jones is adamant that we are saved by a particular kind of grace. He says it is "the grace of God in and through his Son, Jesus Christ, by the grace of the Holy Spirit" (2 Cor. 13:14). In other words, we are made holy, not by our holy actions, but by the actions and life of the Savior (John 1:16). The only way we receive holiness that can maintain a relationship with God the Father is through the union to his Son by the indwelling of the Holy Spirit.

Jones argues that our faith unites us to the person of Christ through the Holy Spirit.[xviii]

We thus participate in Jesus' holiness, which allows us to access a relationship with God the Father. Never is this relationship conditioned upon personal holiness. However, a personal union to Christ will produce evidence of Christ's holiness in our daily actions, thoughts, and words. This is critical to understanding Jesus' demands for disciples.

It is important to emphasize this point: *our personal obedience does not earn our status before God, but rather our relationship to Jesus empowers our obedience.* When we surrender and put our faith in Jesus Christ, he opens every cavern of our ambitions, desires, thoughts, actions, and dreams.

What then is the cost of this relationship? Nothing. And yet, everything.

Discipleship Costs Nothing

The cost of discipleship is nothing.

The only thing required is faith in Jesus Christ and we will be saved (John 3:16, 6:28-29; 1 John 3:23). But you might say, faith isn't nothing! Having faith is still something. However, it is only costly if you have to pay or give something to receive it. Faith doesn't work that way. Faith comes as a gift given by God (Eph. 2:8). Christ cannot be coerced into giving this gift, it comes only from an overflow of grace upon those whom he has chosen (Eph. 1:3-5). The sinner has no means of bartering with God. He cannot offer up a fresh platter of obedience hoping God will delight in his fruits of service. He is plagued with his sinfulness (Rom. 3:23). He cannot make a deal for forgiveness, for there is nothing he can offer to God that God does not already have.

A true disciple thinks, speaks, and acts out of an acute understanding that their discipleship costs nothing.

In Acts 9, Paul, then Saul, was going to Damascus to beat some Christians and throw them in prison. But Jesus revealed Himself to Saul. Jesus told Ananias in Acts 9:15-16, "Go, for he is a chosen instrument of mine to carry my name before the Gentiles and kings and the children of Israel. For I will show Him how much he must suffer for the sake of my name." Paul wasn't chosen to be a disciple of Christ because he had cleaned up his act, started attending a local church, and chose to give up smoking and drinking. Nothing he did made him eligible to be shown grace and forgiveness. But Paul recognized God's grace, and it broke his calloused religious heart and changed his entire life.

As a disciple of Christ, Paul thought through everything with a mind of grace. Paul saw his position as an apostle or servant of Christ due to the will of God (Eph. 1:1, 2 Cor. 1:1, Phil 1:1, Col 1:1). Life revolves not around lists of to dos and not to dos, but the person of Christ (Phil. 1:21-26, 3:7-11). Paul saw himself as having been crucified with Christ, and now his life existed as a conduit for Christ to live through (Gal 2:20). Paul understood he did not earn his discipleship and he could not forfeit it, because it is held by the grace of God (Romans 8:37-39). A true understanding of discipleship produces a mind of humility that is compelled to a continual reliance on the person and work of Jesus.

Discipleship by grace that costs nothing also produces an undeniable change in our speech. Consider Peter on Pentecost in Acts 2. No longer does he cower in front of those who could reject and harm him, but publicly proclaims the Messiah to be the risen Jesus Christ. In Acts, when the people realize their error and the seed of grace begins to blossom in their hearts, they ask what they should do.

Peter's response isn't to join your local synagogue, pay 10% of your income, attend their discipleship classes on Friday nights, and make sure you show up every Saturday morning! He says in Acts 2:38-39, "repent and be baptized every one of you in the name of Jesus Christ for the forgiveness of your sins, and you will receive the gift of the Holy Spirit. For the promise is for you and for your children and for all who are far off, everyone whom the Lord our God calls to himself." His message is bold and piercing, because he recognizes that God calls whoever he wills regardless of who the individual is, or what they have done. Our union to Christ through the Holy Spirit produces power and confidence that defies public opinion and perception.

The extent of Peter's understanding of God's free grace increases as he is told that the gospel message is also for the Gentiles. Acts 15:7 says, "Peter stood up and said to them, Brothers, you know that in the early days God made a choice among you, that by my mouth the Gentiles should hear the word of the gospel and believe." Even the Gentiles, no matter whom their mom or dad were, what they did or didn't do, or where they lived or didn't live! The grace of God is for everyone. The cost is nothing and the message is for everyone.

As a disciple's mind changes by grace, so go their actions. After Peter spoke in Acts 2, those who believed "devoted themselves to the apostles' teaching and the fellowship, to the breaking of bread and the prayers" (Acts 2:42). Those who believed were devoted. This can be defined as "to continue to do something with intense effort, with the possible implication of despite difficulty."[xix] They soaked up the truth and were intentional about being with each other.

When grace grasps a disciple, they have no other option but to respond with action. Not only were they fervently learning, but also giving. In Acts 2:45, it says that "they were selling their possessions and belongings and distributing the proceeds to all, as any had need." Throughout the rest of the New Testament, we see examples of the apostles, Barnabas, Timothy, Titus, Philemon, Priscilla, and Aquila, and many others praised for their actions of faith by Christ's grace.

God's unmerited favor completely compels the believer to change their mind, tongue, and actions. For the outsider looking at the changing life of the believer, they might see great costs and sacrifices being made. Yet, the new saint will simply respond that they are not giving up anything or paying any dues. They are doing what they desire, to serve Jesus. Therefore, the theological and practical reality for the believer is that discipleship costs them nothing. As a result of God's grace, they are now doing what brings them the greatest joy.

Have you grasped the reality of the grace of Jesus Christ? Do you wake up with a crisp mental awareness of your positional holiness before God due to your union to Christ through the Holy Spirit? Is your speech changed by your understanding of what Christ has done for you? If someone was just to walk with you throughout the day and observe your actions, would they see the conduct of a person in humble awe of what God has done for them? Discipleship costs nothing, and once that is properly understood, it changes everything.

I remember being utterly miserable. I was sitting in a tent cold, wet, and unmotivated during a Winter Warfare training exercise. It was me and another student in the tent, suffering together the harsh Alaskan winter. Around midnight, during watch, he made a statement I have heard many times. He said, "I just need to get my life together before committing myself to Christ." I am not exactly sure what provoked that thought. Maybe the misery or frostbite got to him. Regardless, that honest little outburst reveals many people's hearts.

Perhaps this statement reflects your own heart, or a close friend or family member. I want to encourage you with what may seem like a not-so-encouraging statement: There is nothing we can do to make ourselves more appealing to Christ or worthy of His sacrifice and grace. To think so diminishes Jesus' sacrifice and undermines His love. Regardless of anyone's current faith commitments, it is crucial to know and understand that Jesus' gift of grace costs us nothing.

I told my friend, there is nothing you can do to earn God's favor, all you can do is throw yourself into the merciful hands of God and let Him do what He will with your life. I explained how His grace is the only thing that can truly allow us and enable us to live for Him. But I did not finish there. I concluded our conversation by throwing a pebble in his shoe. And that is what I want to do for you now. Just put a small little annoying pebble to get you thinking. I said to him, "but make no mistake, though discipleship costs nothing, it also costs everything."

Discipleship Costs Everything

The cost of discipleship is everything.

Jesus does not try to hide the truth from anyone, real discipleship will produce compounding surrender of self. He says, "if anyone comes to me and does not hate his own father and mother and wife and children and brothers and sisters, yes, and even his own life, he cannot be my disciple. Whoever does not bear his own cross and come after me cannot be my disciple."

I am not trying to be over-simplistic. But Jesus says that our love for Him is to triumph over our love for any other relationship. True disciples are public, not private. For Jesus, no part of an individual's life is personal or off-limits. Everything must be surrendered to Him.

Wait, isn't it just the fanatics who live like this? This verse is for the upper-tier Christians, right? You know, the pastors, elders, and crazy people who think they need to sell all their possessions. Yeah, the insane people who preach the gospel from megaphones nailed to their Christian converted ice cream truck are the only ones who believe this, right?

Honestly, some sinful part of me wishes that were the case. But Jesus is speaking to regular people. He requires us to "renounce all that we have" and follow Him. There is no hierarchical structure for requirements of Christian sacrifice. For every disciple, Jesus commands complete life infiltration into every nook and cranny that exists in our small day to day existence.

I remember talking with a teammate one day about God's goodness. Like many of us, he was having difficultly understanding the problem of evil. How could God be all loving and still allow or even orchestrate all the suffering in the world? I entertained the question and went down the theological rabbit hole a bit. After several days of these discussions my friend felt confident in the answers scripture provides on the topic.

Later on, I then asked him the following, "We have talked about the goodness of God in relation to the suffering of the world, but may I ask something a little more personal? What do you think about the goodness of God and His disapproval of your relationship with your girlfriend?"

Naturally, the conversation took an interesting turn. But this is a habit of a post-modern generation. We want to compartmentalize God into the realm of theology, theory, and overall belief. But God will not be put in the corner of our life. He is the rock on which our life is formed. Jesus demands His disciples break up sinful relationships, quit drinking for drunkenness, come clean about stealing from employers, tell people sorry, forgive others, sell possessions, move locations, quit jobs, take new jobs, talk to the hurting, give to the needy, and surrender everything to be used for the glory of God.

Regrettably, when presenting the gospel, we tend to pendulum swing between Legalism and Antinomianism. Either we talk about grace or law, but rarely do we present them in conjunction.

Understand, our gospel-centered discipleship invitation ought to be grace-centered. But if we fail to expound the reality of complete surrender to Christ, we have failed to present the whole message.

I am always curious why we do that? Why do we sometimes cower to tell someone that their entire life must be dedicated to Jesus? Especially if you believe as I do, that grace is a gift from God. When grace is given it will decisively allow the person to move closer to this reality every day. I can only think of two reasons we tend not to mention the cost. First, we fear people's perception of us. And second, we fear our responsibility to live what we speak.

Many times, when I explain to someone that they must surrender everything to Jesus, I feel embarrassed. I consciously think, who am I to make this statement? Just this morning, I know I was self-centered and left for work early to avoid helping with the kids. How can I tell another person what is required of discipleship when I can't even uphold it? At times I am nervous, feeling self-conscious, wondering if the person I am talking to thinks that I am a total nut job or just another religious fanatic.

We combat these wrong and potentially sinful feelings by reminding each other how discipleship costs nothing. We let grace soak our minds, change our speech, and empower us. Grace emboldens us to declare the true words of God. Combining these two realities enables us to speak with sure conviction, boldness, and strength. Yet, simultaneously, presenting that truth in utter humility and awe. Anyone we encounter will only be able to turn from their sin if God calls them and regenerates their heart. Therefore, when we present the gospel, it must include the paradoxical reality that discipleship costs nothing and everything.

When we verbalize that discipleship costs everything, it impresses our dire need for Christ in conversion and sanctification.

My wife Janelle and I tried our best to teach our girls how to feed themselves from a young age. We even tried the baby lead weaning program. We wanted to encourage them to regulate their food despite the natural mess. The kitchen floor looked like the feeding trough from the prize pig at the local fair! So, even though our girls could barely eat a banana before it became mush, we were desperate to have our floor back, thus we quickly introduced utensils.

The first time I gave Maggie a fork, she looked at it and immediately discarded the mysterious item, leaving it to rest on top of the floor feeding trough. Janelle was significantly more patient and gifted at teaching the girls. She put up with much fork throwing and using the wrong end to attempt a bite. Eventually, the girls learned. At ages 4 and 6, they think they are ready for chopsticks. The point is, they didn't get it at first. To my knowledge there is no child protégée with utensils, it just takes time.

Imagine if Janelle just threw in the towel after Maggie or Audrey threw the fork on the ground for the fiftieth time. As parents in this culture, we will teach our children, no matter how frustrating it might be, to eat their food with utensils. Our expectation for them is that they will one day accomplish this task, but we never expect them to be perfect at it the first time.

God expects His children to give everything to Him and pursue perfect holiness. But God never expects us to get it on the 1st try, or the 2nd, or the 470th. God expects His disciples to understand what he commands, and to trust in Him to teach and guide them into one day accomplishing it.

Therefore, discipleship costs nothing. The unmerited favor of God compels the believer to change their mind, tongue, and actions. And yet, discipleship costs everything. It points us to our need for Christ in conversion and continual need in our road to holiness.

The requirements of discipleship never change, it is a total giving of oneself to serve and depend on Jesus every day that he blesses us with. So, what does that look like practically? What does the life of a disciple who is required to give everything but pay nothing look like?

It looks like maximum personal effort combined with absolute dependence on Christ. Effort without dependence is futile, and dependence without effort is false. The imperfect perfect product that comes from utter effort and complete dependence will be a believer S.O.L.D. out for Jesus.

S.O.L.D.

S.O.L.D. is an acronym describing four specific marks that Jesus says will be evident in every true disciple's life. They define the character of a disciple and provide a helpful way for us to measure and assess our own discipleship. A true disciple of Jesus Christ will Sacrifice, Obey, Love and Disciple others by their heart motivated dependence and service to Jesus. These four concepts come straight from the teachings of Jesus and are compatible and supportive of each other. By studying, internalizing, and practicing these four characteristics, we actively keep our minds Christocentric. Each mark serves as a mirror for us to look at and analyze our own walk with Christ.

When a disciple is united to Jesus through the indwelling of the Holy Spirit they will display evidences of Sacrifice, Obedience, Love, and the Discipling of others. I believe these four marks provide a helpful way for us to take an introspective look at our own walk with Jesus. Each mark represents a major theme of scripture. Jesus doesn't make these statements in passing. Each one is tied to a biblical theme that is woven through every page of scripture. The rest of this book will examine these themes of scripture and their marks on disciples.

Summary

My hope is that the remainder of this book will be a rich study of scripture and God's desire for your life. As you read through the following chapters, remember that to be a disciple costs nothing and everything. No amount of work you can perform will make God love you any more than he already does. And there is no limit to His demands upon your life. Rest confident in His power to sustain you to do precisely what He desires of you. Yet, read with a heart open to the Spirit's conviction of what He may be asking of you.

Throughout the rest of the book, It will give two chapters to the study of each mark of a disciple. The first will trace the theological significance of that mark, mainly in the Old Testament. The second will examine the theme predominately in the New Testament and break down what it looks like for us today.

We start first with Sacrifice.

Chapter 3: Sacrifice

Theological Significance of Sacrifice

"The multitude of your sacrifices-- what are they to me?" says the LORD. "I have more than enough of burnt offerings, of rams and the fat of fattened animals; I have no pleasure in the blood of bulls and lambs and goats." - Isaiah 1:11

My first thought was this can't be real. There is simply no universe where I could imagine what my ears were hearing to be true. I stood there in a stupor as our guide continued to explain this ancient ferocious game. As he was speaking, I stared down at my feet. I was standing on the floor of the Madison Square Garden equivalent 2000 years ago. When I looked around, I saw astonishing stone architecture that surrounded a rectangular arena a little smaller than a football field. A few thousand years ago a game was played on this stone covered arena that is completely backward to anything a western mind could ever understand.

This game was played by young men up to the age of 18. They were selected randomly from the nation's tribes. These high school age boys would practice this game all year. It was their hope to be selected to play in the year end celebratory game. It was intriguing how the game was played, even though it was quite simple. Kick, head butt, or throw a ball through vertical holes on the side of a wall. There were referees with basic rules and such, but for the most part, it was a full contact battle to see who could win. At the end of the game, the winning team had an enormous celebration and were greatly honored amongst the whole community.

Just like at the super bowl every year, this people group would elect an MVP (Most Valuable Player). Typically, this was the guy with the most goals. His proven worth and achievement made him an instant celebrity. He became the focal point for the entire people group. Everyone would shout his name, cheer, and throw flowers. He was hoisted onto the shoulders of other men and paraded amongst the people.

Next comes the most unbelievable part. This young man's reward for his sacrifice was to become a living sacrifice. They would bring him to the top of the temple and begin praising the gods. They brought their best young man before them. After strapping him to the cold stone alter, they proceeded to mutilate him. One of the greatest honors a young Mayan man lived for was to be the victor and consequently, a human sacrifice.

Call it primitive, grotesque, inhuman, unimaginable, barbaric, or whatever other titles you want. Was their belief misplaced and tragic? Without question. But consider the contrast. These people competed for the honor and opportunity to give their lives for their false gods. We who have God's very word, clear historical evidence, a legacy of faith in the one true God, have difficulty sacrificing Sunday Football, let alone becoming a sacrifice. We struggle to open our lips to praise our creator and savior out of fear of embarrassment. We wrestle with what number to write on a check for those servants who live to administer God's Word. We are more concerned with the affection and admiration of others than we are God's. We prioritize our comfort over obeying God's commands. Incorrectly or not, Christians have become a people labeled by our neighbors as hypocritical, two-faced, arrogant, self-righteous, and bigots.

We cannot call ourselves disciples of Christ without tangible life sacrifice. To follow Christ is to follow His sacrificial example.

Throughout the redemption story, sacrifice has played and will play a crucial role in our complete reconciliation to the father.

In this chapter, we will explore the historical context and progression of sacrificial worship amongst Old Testament Patriarchs and Israel. What we find is that true sacrifice is only beneficial when action and faith work together in unison.

Biblical Sacrificial Beginnings

You and I likely grew up in different cultural settings. As mentioned, I grew up in the Pacific Northwest, just on the outskirts of Seattle. In Seattle, it wasn't common practice to go out and slaughter baby lambs to worship God and atone for sin. I am pretty sure they can arrest you for that sort of thing. After all, we are a city where pets have seating sections at local restaurants. The only animal sacrifice we are familiar with is a good ole barbeque.

Historic ritualistic sacrifice can be difficult to understand. Why does God command such brutality? These are important questions for us to ask. For, to rightly understand Jesus' sacrifice and His call for His disciples to sacrifice, we need to grasp the Old Testament's perspective on it. Consider then with me the biblical history of sacrifice.

Before we start, this is not meant to be a complete biblical theology on sacrifice. Massive scholarly works have already done that. This overview is meant to ensure we understand the big picture of scripture on sacrifice so we can accurately understand Jesus' sacrifice. With that stipulation, we begin with the fruit and two naked people.

In the beginning, there was no sacrifice. We were created to know God and enjoy Him and His creation. Adam and Eve lived in perfect harmony with God and creation. They ate all the variety of vegetation in the garden while walking and talking with the Lord in paradise. All that they knew was the goodness of God and the enjoyment of life. All of that changed when sin entered the world.

Sin penetrated the union between God and man and severed it. God pronounced that man would die since they disobeyed his command and ate from the tree of the knowledge of good and evil. However, in His grace, God did not immediately strike Adam and Eve dead when they disobeyed. Instead, He removed earthly eternal life and made their days numbered. Humanity must now also work and toil to gather food to sustain themselves. Yet, even during this sentence, God presents a future hope in their decedents.

He gives them the protoevangelion, the first gospel. In Genesis 3:15, God speaks to the serpent, "I will put enmity between you and the woman, and between your offspring and her offspring; he shall bruise your head, and you shall bruise his heel." Essentially, God is foretelling Adam and Eve that one day, a Son would be born and destroy Satan. This marks the beginning of the two seeds of humanity. That of the serpent and the woman.

From this point on, sacrifice plays a critical role in redemptive history. At first, it is called in Hebrew הַמִּנְחָ (Minhah), it can mean several things, but predominately refers to an offering. It is this word that is used to reference Cain and Abel's gifts to God. From the beginning, there are distinctions made between individual's sacrifices. God delights in one and disregards another.

Cain and Abel

The story is found in Genesis 4:1-16. The two main characters are brothers, sons of Adam and Eve. Cain worked in the garden and Abel in the fields with the sheep. Now before you meat lovers try to take shots at our vegetarian brothers and sisters, God's favor isn't a reflection of the type of sacrifice. Acceptance of sacrifice concerns the heart and motivation of the one presenting it. Look at what happens when Cain hears of God's reaction. Genesis 4:5 says, "So Cain was very angry, and his face fell." Cain is ticked. He is slaving away in this thistle ridden garden thanks to Dad. He tries to make amends to God by giving Him the produce of his hard work, and God doesn't even care! On the other hand, God is pleased with Abel, his sheep lover of a brother. Why? The Word gives us at least two reasons.

First, Cain's conduct was already evil. 1 John 3:12 explains that Cain "was of the evil one and murdered his brother. And why did he murder him? Because his deeds were evil and his brother's righteous." Cain wasn't a good guy who made a bad decision. His deeds were already corrupt before his savage act against his brother.

Second, Cain's sacrifice was faithless. In Hebrews 11:4 it says "By faith, Abel offered to God a more acceptable sacrifice than Cain, through which he was commended as righteous, God commending him by accepting his gifts. And through his faith, though he died, he still speaks." Abel came to God in total belief and faith in the power and rule of God. As Abraham in Gen. 15:6 was credited righteousness due to his faith, so was Abel. God's disregard of Cain's sacrifice was a statement upon the faithlessness with which Cain offered it.

Genesis 4:6 continues with the story. Cain is on his face in open rage when God says to him, "Why are you angry, and why has your face fallen? If you do well, will you not be accepted? And if you do not do well, sin is crouching at the door. Its desire is contrary to you, but you must rule over it." God comes to Cain despite Cain's response. Amazingly, God is graciously ready and wanting to accept Cain. No matter how much we mess things up, God is always ready and willing to accept us when we are ready to submit to Him. However, Cain did not choose to listen.

This first example teaches us that the acceptance of sacrifice is conditioned upon *faith* that results in *action*. A principle we shall see repeated throughout scripture as we investigate their interconnectivity.

Noah and Abraham

The next example God's word gives us on offerings is with Noah. Genesis 8:20 says "Then Noah built an altar to the LORD and took some of every clean animal and some of every clean bird and offered burnt offerings on the altar." Noah here isn't butchering one of all the different kinds of animals he brought, that would be a bit counterproductive to the whole two by two idea. Nor is Noah being over the top righteous, he is simply doing what God has instructed him to do.

In Gen. 7:2 God says, "take with you seven pairs of all clean animals, the male and his mate, and a pair of the animals that are not clean, the male and his mate." Therefore, God instructed Noah before the flood ever began to be prepared to provide a sacrifice for when God delivered him.

This is an interesting turn. Here sacrificial offering is scripted into the plan as a way of confirming God will do what He says. Imagine God being the General of an army about to go into a battle where they are significantly outnumbered and outmatched. God is in effect saying to His men, get the celebratory feast prepared and ready before we go. Prep each soldiers seat and plate. Do not be negligent in the preparation. For we are going to win this fight and I will bring you all back safely. No one shall be harmed. In this instance, sacrifice is as much praise of God's preparation as it is a praise of His deliverance.

By sacrificing these animals Noah is declaring his dependence and trust in the Lord to provide and carry out his plan for humanity.

Do you think it is logical to sacrifice these animals? Sure you have a male and female of each kind still left over. But what if one of those two dies? Then the entire species is extinct! Sacrifice is about faith, resulting in action, submitting to oneself to God's plan. His plan is what He desires and determines, and not according to whether Noah or anyone else thinks it is a good idea or not.

Abraham and Isaac provide another distinct example of sacrificial worship. Similarly, we see that sacrifice is accepted when faith results in action. Again, we see praise in both preparation and execution of the action of sacrifice.

In Genesis God tests Abraham in the most insane way. Genesis 22:1-2 states, "After these things God tested Abraham and said to him, "Abraham!" And he said, "Here I am." ² He said, "Take your son, your only son Isaac, whom you love, and go to the land of Moriah, and offer him there as a burnt offering on one of the mountains of which I shall tell you." I know you Lord of the Rings fans just geeked out at the name Moriah, it's okay I did too, but try to stay focused.

God is asking Abraham for his complete self. God wants all of Abraham's heart, trust, dependency, and love. The way God tests this, is to ask Abraham to sacrifice the one thing he has waited years for and loves deeply, his only son. If you aren't familiar with the story or need a quick refresher, remember this is the son that was promised to Abraham years ago when God first called him in Genesis 12. But he and his wife were barren until God miraculously allowed Sarah to become pregnant in her old age of almost 100 years. This was the child that God would cause a nation to arise from and bless the world through. And now God is commanding Abraham to offer that child to Him. Abraham's response is wild:

"So Abraham rose early in the morning, saddled his donkey, and took two of his young men with him, and his son Isaac. And he cut the wood for the burnt offering and arose and went to the place of which God had told him. ⁴On the third day, Abraham lifted up his eyes and saw the place from afar. ⁵Then Abraham said to his young men, "Stay here with the donkey; I and the boy will go over there and worship and come again to you" - Genesis 22:3-6

Several things are important to note. The first is that we again see an act of faith in God's promises in the preparation of this sacrifice. God's covenant with Abraham rests upon this boy's life. If he dies, so dies the promises God has given to Abraham. Thus, in cutting wood, saddling the donkeys, and taking a three-day journey, Abraham is declaring his trust and allegiance to God. He is praising God in how he prepares to sacrifice.

Second, Abraham sees no contradiction between God's command and God's promise. He tells his servants that they both will return. In Hebrews 11:19 the author under inspiration interprets this to mean that Abraham "considered that God was able even to raise him from the dead."

Third, Abraham demonstrates his complete surrender to the will of God when he executes his decisive action to give Isaac as a sacrifice. As he is about to offer up his boy, "the angel of the LORD called to him from heaven and said, "Abraham, Abraham...Do not lay your hand on the boy or do anything to him, for now, I know that you fear God, seeing you have not withheld your son, your only son, from me."

Sacrifice is a physical demonstration of an inward conviction.

This event accomplished several things in the life of Abraham. First, he demonstrated his verbal allegiance to God by faith resulting in physical action. In doing so he also proved to himself the sincerity of his own belief. As human beings, we can make grand boasts of what we are willing to do but often do not follow through. Abraham did.

Second, he cemented God's provision in his son's mind. Imagine being tied down on firewood and having your Dad stand over you with a knife, ready to sacrifice you to God. That will burn an image in your mind.

Isaac would never forget that day. His father so believed the Lord that he was willing to obey whatever he asked. Isaac witnessed how the Lord provided the offering for that trip. He provided a substitutionary lamb for Abraham to offer in Isaac's place. Though Isaac did not understand it then, he participated in a picture of the glorious gospel that would come from his descendant, Jesus Christ. As God provided a lamb as a substitute for Isaac so God has sent His Son, whom He loves, as a substitute for us.

In sacrifice, we worship God in both preparation and physical action. In the previous example of Abraham and Isaac, we are also introduced to how there is a substitutionary element to sacrifice. This concept of atonement becomes central as God's revelation continues to His servant Moses.

Moses and Sinai

Up until the time of Moses, there was no written description of how God ought to be worshiped. Everything had been passed down orally. However, after 400 years passed from Abraham to the time of Moses, Israel had grown close to 1 or 2 million living as slaves in Egypt. When God brings them out of slavery, he instructs them on how they will live as a theocracy, a God-centered society. A major part of this theocracy is the formal institution of sacrificial worship.

Before we jump into the law and the many various types of sacrifices, let's address the immediate question: Why all the blood, cutting, and carnage? For those who have read through the Bible you are already aware of the explicit graphic nature of sacrifices contained in Exodus and Leviticus. Why didn't people have to do this before Mt. Sinai?

The simple answer is righteousness, as demonstrated with Abraham, has always been credited based upon faith.

However, now Israel has become a significant sized people. And a holy God cannot dwell amongst an unholy people. The reason isn't that God is going to be affected in some negative way by people's sin, quite the opposite. People's sin will not be tolerated long in the presence of the Lord before the He administers His justice. If an unholy people are going to live with God, then they must purify themselves regularly. Therefore, ceremonial removal of sin from the people enabled them to live in proximity to God. To do this, He provided for His people substitutionary sacrificial atonement.

The sacrificial system does not only cover sin offerings. Sixty percent of the sacrifices can be voluntary acts of worship. So, man does not approach God however he sees fit or in whatever manner is comfortable to Him. God prescribes His worship. God declares how He is to be praised, worshipped, and thanked. And for Israel, the primary way a grateful and joyful heart was expressed is through sacrifice. Within God's sacrificial system there are five different types of sacrifices addressed.

The first sacrifice is the burnt offering. Leviticus opens by discussing the nature of the burnt offering. The sacrifice selected from the herd should have no defect and the entire animal is the Lord's (Lev. 1). Presenting a burnt offering could be done as a voluntary act of worship, an atonement for sin, a general expression of devotion, or a declared commitment to God's calling or plan.

The second sacrifice is the grain offering. This is an offering of the harvest that is often due to a voluntary act of worship. Most often this is to praise God for His provision or is part of a pledge of devotion. The priest was instructed to consume the remainder of the offering after it had been presented to the Lord (Lev. 2, 6-14-23).

The third sacrifice is the peace offering. Here the worshiper brings a sacrifice as a form of praise, thanksgiving, or simply free will. Additionally, this could be found in ceremonial meals. Leviticus 3 and 7 gives further information. At times this offering would be given after the fulfillment of a vow.

The fourth sacrifice is the sin offering. This sacrifice is discussed more than any other. It is required for anyone found in sin. Sin is "that which is an offense against a standard."[xx] This is the only sacrifice with economic provision. Depending on the worshiper's financial status they are required to offer either a bull, male goat, female goat, dove or pigeon, or 1/10 ephah of fine flour for the very poor. The sacrifice for the repentant worshiper provides the means of their atonement and forgiveness before God. We will revisit this sacrifice in greater detail in the following chapter.

The fifth sacrifice is the trespass offering. Essentially this offering had to be made anytime there was a sin committed where something was damaged, and restitution had to be made (Lev. 5:14-19). Therefore, not only was a ram required for sacrifice but full restitution fitting to the situation had to be given.

The common denominator is all these sacrifices had specific reasons and processes for being offered. God does not give the worshipper permission to deter from His prescription. Should one do so, there are fatal consequences.

Aaron's sons, unfortunately, are an example of this reality. Leviticus 10:1 says, "now Nadab and Abihu, the sons of Aaron, each took his censer and put fire in it and laid incense on it and offered unauthorized fire before the LORD, which he had not commanded them." In other translations, the word "unauthorized" is translated as "strange." The fire that Aaron's sons constructed was their creation and not according to the instruction that God commanded. The result was "fire came out from before the LORD and consumed them, and they died before the Lord." God has made it clear from the beginning of sacrificial law, that to deviate from His prescription is an act of disregard for His commandments, and will not go unpunished. This ill-fated example cemented the seriousness necessarily for Israel to possess when they come to worship the only true, holy, and great God.

Action and faith must accompany all forms of sacrificial worship. To depart from either the action or the sincere belief in the purpose of the action is to breach God's instruction. God will not be mocked, disregarded, or manipulated by insincere worship.

The Prophets

The prophets teach us a different vantage point on sacrifice. They correct the misconception that sacrifice is merely an activity. Acceptable sacrifice must be done in faith that results in action. Simply conducting the action apart from faith is useless.

The prophet Isaiah writes in 1:11-12, "What to me is the multitude of your sacrifices? says the LORD; I have had enough of burnt offerings of rams and the fat of well-fed beasts; I do not delight in the blood of bulls, or of lambs, or of goats... bring me no more vain offerings." Israel continued to obey the law through sacrificial atonement for sin, but there was no remorse or guilt or desire to turn from their sin. Instead, they decided in their hearts to sin against the Lord and then simply offer a sacrifice in obedience to His law. This is further revealed in Isaiah 29:13 when the prophet quotes the Lord saying, "because this people draw near with their mouth and honor me with their lips, while their hearts are far from me, and their fear of me is a commandment taught by men."

I was still in the beginning stages of my military training. Like a middle school student looking for what mom or dad didn't say, my class eagerly and creatively sought ways to accomplish a task as efficiently as possible. I remember during a specific block of training where the common punishment was to jump in the chilly Pacific Ocean. The punishment took the form of two verbal commands, "hit the surf" and "get wet." Being wet was the worst. There wasn't much wiggle room with "hit the surf", you pretty much had to run to the ocean. However, one day we discovered we could accomplish the task to "get wet" while avoiding the brisk ocean and the extra run to get there. We ran around a building out of view, then doubled back to a barracks where we took a rushed 10-second hot shower. Then we hurriedly ran back to receive the rest of our sadistic punishments. Did we accomplish the task? Absolutely!

Israel thought they could pull one over on God. They became desensitized. Instead of belief, they became devoted to duty and tradition. They tried to manipulate God's rules to serve their sinful purposes. They thought they could accomplish a command in a way other than what God had declared. They simply forgot who God is.

They forgot about His aseity, that He is from Himself and needs nothing. Paul says in Acts 17:24-25, "The God who made the world and everything in it, being Lord of heaven and earth, does not live in temples made by man, 25 nor is he served by human hands, as though he needed anything, since he himself gives to all mankind life and breath and everything." John Frame helps us understand this, stating that sacrificial worship "in the OT was not to satiate God's hunger, but symbolically to atone for human sin... we offer thanks for the fact that God has met our needs. Through vows, we incur our obligations to him. And we call him to meet our needs in the future."[xxi] Israel thought they could earn God's blessing by stale religious action apart from transformed faith. They were wrong. There is only one acceptable demeanor, utter and complete sincere surrender.

The prophet Malachi shows what this faithlessness looked like. He says in 1:6-8:

"A son honors his father, and a servant his master. If then I am a father, where is my honor? And if I am a master, where is my fear? says the LORD of hosts to you, O priests, who despise my name. But you say, 'How have we despised your name?' ⁷ By offering polluted food upon my altar. But you say, 'How have we polluted you?' By saying that the LORD's table may be despised. ⁸ When you offer blind animals in sacrifice, is that not evil? And when you offer those that are lame or sick, is that not evil? Present that to your governor; will he accept you or show you favor?"

Israel tried to do the minimum. Their faith in God had lapsed which resulted in faulty actions. They tried to reinterpret God's word to suit their own desires. Such an attitude is not reflective of a person who sincerely fears and loves the gracious Alpha and Omega creator.

God is blunt with His feelings for those who approach His worship in such a manner. He continues, "Oh that there were one among you who would shut the doors, that you might not kindle fire on my altar in vain! I have no pleasure in you, says the LORD of hosts, and I will not accept an offering from your hand" (Mal. 1:10). Sacrificial worship is vital and commanded, but cannot be faked or performed. Our King will only accept genuine faithful action.

Are you willing to defend the pure worship of God in such a manner that you would shut the churches doors? Sacrificial worship requires the sacrifice of both possession and reputations. The disciple must desire the praise and worship of God over that of people.

Summary

From the first sacrifice, God has made clear He requires both our hands and our hearts. Sacrifice is not about giving something to God that He needs. Sacrifice is about God giving to us what we need. We need a tangible physical way of worshiping Him and atonement for sin. In the Old Testament, sacrifice provides temporary atonement and foreshadows the final future in Jesus. But God is never manipulated or coaxed into performance. Sacrificial worship is only received when the worshiper comes before the Holy God with genuine faith that results in specific action.

If you claim faith in God, has your faith resulted in action? Or on the other side, are your actions rooted in faith? I think many of us tend to think going to church, giving a tithe, praying before meals, reading the bible, attending a men's or women's group, and being an all-around nice person is the standard for a good Christian. Is it possible we have fallen into a similar situation as Israel during the time of Isaiah?

Perhaps, we have accumulated a multitude of actions that have resulted from tradition, duty, and what is accepted by society rather than faith? Let me ask this. Did you pray before your last meal? If you did, why did you do it? What was the substance of your prayer? Was it the same thing you pray before every meal? Is it possible that your prayer was out of tradition and duty rather than actual thanksgiving to God?

Take this moment as an opportunity to consider the daily or weekly sacrificial actions you do for God. Write them down on a piece of paper or create a note in your phone. List everything you can think of. Write down any instance where you sacrifice time, money, energy, or materials for God. Once you have them written down, observe each occurrence over the next day or week. Analyze your heart motivation in those moments. Are you sacrificing because of your genuine faith and love for God or out of duty, obligation, and tradition? Wrestle with these aspects before moving on to the cross in the next chapter.

At the cross many truths we discover in the Old Testament are forever and irreversibly changed. However, we will see in this next chapter the principles of sacrificial worship remain the same. Genuine faith results in specific action. We also find in the crucifixion of Christ, the fulfillment and finest expression of sacrificial worship.

Chapter 4: Sacrifice

A True Disciple will Sacrifice

"The world values power, comfort, success, and recognition. Jesus frees us to value grief, sacrifice, weakness, and exclusion." - Tim Keller

Her day is filled with a fundamental commitment to sacrificial worship. When she wakes up, her thoughts go immediately to preparing the temple for the worship service that day. Her motivation at times wains, but she always finds a way to complete the task so that no blemish is noticeable in the sanctuary. With care, love, and true sincerity she prepares the food offering for her god. Careful not to burn or undercook the offertory meal she practices discipline in her craft.

Once the offering has been accepted, many times without any recognition, she humbly surrenders her time to transport her god to the places it desires. Though she may have worries, doubts, concerns, and insecurities, her duty and continual sacrifice are unquestioned. This is just a few hours of her morning. She does this every day and much more out of her sincere and utter love for her god.

Her name is Mother. The temple is the Home. The preparation is her diligence in managing the home. She tirelessly serves her family, often without any recognition. And her god is her children. She will give until she gives the ultimate sacrifice to see them happy, healthy, and successful.

This simple little parable could easily have been of any man or woman who places anything else on the throne except God.

People practice sacrificial worship every day. Sacrificial worship surrounds us and has invaded every conceivable area of life. But instead of labeling it sacrificial worship, we call it discipline, healthy living, climbing the ladder, sports fanatic, financial security, or helicopter parent. Every person, every day, is sacrificing for the thing that they believe will bring them fulfillment in life.

In the last chapter, we saw how God has given us the ability to sacrifice as a tangible way to worship Him and atone for sin. We saw how genuine faith results in specific action. Sadly, in life, we often sacrifice for the wrong thing. We perhaps can be deceived into thinking we are sacrificing for God, when it is really for ourselves. It can be hard to discern if our motivation in sacrifice is truly for God or something else.

If you did your homework you observed the different things you sacrifice on a daily or weekly basis. What was your assessment of your motivations? Was there anything that surprised you? Keep the answers to these questions in your mind as you read through this next chapter, because we are going to examine the cross and how it transforms our motivations.

We already looked in chapter 2 at how Jesus declares a true disciple will sacrifice. However, our definition of sacrifice is forever changed on the cross. If we focus our gaze on how the cross changed sacrifice, something marvelous happens. The disciple finds assurance, confidence, motivation, and true joy in personal sacrificial worship.

The Cross Changed Everything

The true Christian's understanding of sacrificial worship is derived from their theology of the cross. What happened to Jesus

Christ on the cross is vital to every decision we make. The cross changes how we understand our position before God and how we live our life for Him and to Him. The cross sets a new standard for our sacrifice. However, just as a sacrifice was only accepted through genuine faith resulting in specific action in the OT, the same remains true post-cross. So, what exactly happened on the cross?

Per Wayne Grudem, Jesus met four of humanities needs on the cross.[xxii]

The first of these needs is a sacrifice. In chapter 3, we looked intently at how God had given Israel animal sacrifice to worship Him and atone for sin. On the cross, often called the Great Exchange, Jesus took upon Himself our sin and imputed to us His righteousness. As Hebrews 9:26 says, "He has appeared once for all at the end of the age to put away sin by the sacrifice of himself." Jesus took our place on the cross and died the sinner's death. He became the sacrifice that we desperately needed.

This leads to the second need, propitiation. Jesus removes God's wrath from us. Romans 3:23 tells us that the wages for our sin is death. We deserve God's just wrathful punishment. But Christ became our propitiation. 1 John 4:10 says, "In this is love, not that we loved God, but that he loved us and sent His son to be the propitiation for our sins." God retains no more wrath against a disciple of Christ. No action can undo what Jesus has done.

Thirdly, Jesus has reconciled us back into a right relationship with the Father. God is not indifferent toward the followers of Christ, but He is pleased with us based upon His Son. 2 Corinthians 5:18-19 claims that God, "through Christ reconciled us to Himself and gave us the ministry of reconciliation; that is, in Christ God was reconciling the world to Himself." The only way the Christian can assist in the ministry of reconciliation is if they have been reconciled. We can now confidently proclaim to others that a right relationship with God the Father is possible through Jesus Christ. This brings about the last need, redemption.

Lastly, redemption is where the believer is bought out of slavery. We are no longer slaves to sin but alive to Christ. Jesus paid our penalty and has redeemed us out of a depraved nature to one that is alive to Him. Mark 10:45 says, "For the son of man also came not to be served but to serve, and to give His life as a ransom for many." The disciple of Jesus Christ is redeemed and removed from the rule of Satan, sin, and death.

SACRIFICE → PROPITIATION →

RECONCILIATION → REDEMPTION

The cross satisfies these four essential human needs. There is no more sacrifice we must make, no wrath that must be appeased, no chiasm that separates us, nor bond that holds us away from a loving relationship with our heavenly father. Once a disciple, there is nothing one can do to make God love them anymore or any less then He already does in Jesus. They are complete in Christ. They lack nothing, need nothing, and can give nothing. Everything is satisfied in the person of Jesus Christ!

I believe all the above statements are theologically accurate and defensible through the scriptures. How then does Jesus say, "in the same way, those of you who do not give up everything you have cannot be my disciples" (Luke 14:33). Isn't the work of Jesus Christ completely independent of anything I do? Didn't we just say there was nothing a person can do to improve their position before God? Didn't we prove at the beginning of this book that being a disciple is being a Christian?

Well, it may seem we must do something to be a disciple! We must; give up everything!

What we are seeing in this section of Luke is rather simple. We can do nothing to become a disciple of Jesus Christ except believe in Him, with belief itself being a gift (Eph. 2:8-10), but once we truly believe in Him, we can do nothing but wrestle with the flesh to sacrificially give up everything for Him.

Stated a different way, when we genuinely believe, we naturally desire personal sacrifice.

What Jesus is describing is the outward manifestation of an inward reality. He does not mean that every believer will sell everything, though He does call some to that life. Instead, He is making a clear statement that once a person is a disciple, every area of his or her life is His.

Sacrificial worship is not ritualistic, but centric to Christian living. Sacrificial living will necessarily pour out of the disciple's life due to their new nature in Christ. If this practice is completely absent for an extended period, the genuine conversion and true discipleship of the individual is in question. There is no room for ambiguity here.

A life lived without Christ-centered sacrifice is a life without Christ.

A true disciple will sacrifice.

True Disciples Will Sacrifice

No one calls a giant gaping hole in the ground a lake. There must be some H2O in there to call it a body of water. Without water, you just have a crater, a pit, the Grand Canyon, a valley, or a mega huge hole in the earth.

Call a person without sacrifice whatever you want. But you cannot call them a true disciple of Jesus. I will add the qualification that I am not referring to backsliding true born again Christians, but rather to individuals who say they believe in Christ but have no Christ-centered sacrificial evidence in their life. What does this Christ-centered sacrifice look like on this side of the cross?

Essentially it can be broken down into the idea inherent in sacrifice's theme verse. Luke 14:26 says, "If anyone comes to me and does not hate his father and mother and wife and children and brothers and sisters, yes, and even his own life, he cannot be my disciple." To hate here is emphatic for love less. Or to phrase it positively, we must love Christ more than any other thing or relationship in our lives. Christ-centered sacrificial worship is to follow Christ's action and give our very selves to God.

The other day I was in the gym listening to Trevor Joy at The Village Church preach a message and something struck me in the analogy he used.[xxiii] Trevor used the account of Elizabeth Elliot watching her son being baptized by the man who speared her husband to death, as a way of discussing vivification and healing. But when he quoted Elizabeth Elliot's penned words, all I could think was here are the beautiful transformed words of a genuine heartfelt disciple.

Trevor quoted Elizabeth who wrote, "To forgive is to die. It is to give up one's right to self, which is precisely what Jesus requires of anyone who wants to be his disciple." She went on to quote Mark 8:35, "If anyone wants to follow in my footsteps, he must give up all right to himself, take up his cross and follow me. For the man who wants to save his life will lose it; but the man who loses his life for my sake will find it."

Elizabeth demonstrated the essence of sacrifice, which is death. Death to self. You may be thinking right now, "I am not ready to sacrifice like that. I can't even forgive the jerk who cut me off in traffic, let alone forgive the man who murdered my family member." I think 90% of us are in that boat. I am still having trouble with terrible thoughts toward the guy who put a ticket on my dash for being two minutes over my parking meter. Christ does not demand we be exactly as we ought, but that we strive to act according to what we are, born again children of God.

Take Peter as an example. Everyone loves to talk about Peter, and it's not hard to see why. The dude is irritably relatable, because we all have had Peter moments.

In Matthew 16:13-23. Jesus asks the disciples who they think he is and Peter replies, "You are the Christ, the Son of the living God." Jesus praises Peter, "Blessed are you, Simon Bar-Jonah! For flesh and blood has not revealed this to you, but my Father who is in heaven." Jesus doesn't stop there but tells Peter that he will receive a set of keys to the kingdom of heaven. I remember the feeling when my Dad handed me the keys to our 1990 Chevy Suburban. I thought I had won the lottery. Imagine getting the keys to heaven!

As quickly as Peter is praised, he is reprimanded. The next section in Matthew 16 records Peter responding to Jesus' announcement of His imminent death. Peter says, "Far be it from you, Lord! This shall never happen to you." Then Jesus counters, "get behind me, Satan! You are a hindrance to me. For you are not setting your mind on the things of God, but on the things of man."

The 180 degree change we see in Matthew 16 with Peter is what some of us experience daily. In the morning you wake up, have a quiet time, and pray to the sovereign God of the universe. You shout His praises silently as you thumb through His word and drink your morning 100% Arabica coffee. After a wonderful time thanking the Lord and making requests on behalf of His Kingdom, you head off to start your day. Within 15 minutes you are frustrated on your phone trying to dodge cars as you weave in and out of traffic. You murder the jerk who cuts you off on the road by hating him in your heart. You are immediately convicted, try to repent, realize you're still hating the guy, and end up trying to repent all the way to work!

By the time you show up to work all you want to do is get the day over with so you can beat traffic home, not kill anyone else in your heart, get a little yard work done, and maybe catch the end of your favorite show or sports game. But when you get home, there is a to-do list, a text message from your budget software saying you went over in one category. Oh and guess what! You ran out of data for the month on your phone plan. Plus, you forgot to respond to a work email, so now your boss needs you. After changing in the room, you look next to your bed and there are a bunch of thank you cards you still haven't written. After dinner, you are trying to clean up only to find out you didn't unload the dishwasher from this morning. On top of all that, the kids are living examples of the depravity of man and bedtime is a disaster. Okay, perhaps this is more my average day then it is yours, but I am sure you can relate.

Isn't it amazing, you can start so focused on the things of God, only to finish completely dominated by the things of man! Christian life looks like a heart monitor. The ups and downs of our day to day lives are just proof that we are alive. The goal is to put that monitor at an angle. As a result, every low isn't quite as low as the last and every high is a little higher than the previous. Imagine it like a mountain range leading up to the pinnacle peak. During the climb, there will always be setbacks. There will be valleys to go down and false summits to climb, but every step is still another step toward the final point, the haystack, the apex, the top, the final summit.

Sacrificial worship is the Christian's proof of a redeemed pulse. In sacrificial worship, we demonstrate ourselves to be genuine disciples of Christ. Though the goal is always perfection, the high points do not save us, and the low points do not condemn us. Instead, both the high and low points should produce repentance, praise, worship, petition, and thanksgiving that we are accepted by God in the state that we are. The heart that strives to live sacrificially for Christ is proof of genuine discipleship.

A Disciple's Heartbeat

At the cross, Jesus changed everything. Nothing we do can save us, and yet how we live proves or disproves our genuine conversion. If there is a real disciple's heartbeat within us, then we will seek to sacrifice. So, what does this sacrificial worship look like? How do we examine our lives to see if we are indeed evidencing a striving heart of sacrifice?

Sacrifice of Family

This has already been discussed, but let's look further at what Jesus calls us to sacrifice regarding our family. Luke 14:25 says clearly, "If anyone comes to me and does not hate his own father and mother and wife and children and brothers and sisters, yes, and even his own life, he cannot be my disciple." The expression is phrased negatively for the emphatic meaning. Everyone else must be loved less than Jesus. A true disciple must love Jesus above all other relationships. Jesus explains it like this in Matt. 10:37 "Whoever loves father or mother more than me is not worthy of me, and whoever loves son or daughter more than me is not worthy of me." No one can love someone more than Christ and still be His disciple.

Let's be clear, to love Christ is not to hate our families and friends. When we love Christ as we ought to then we are given a love for those around us that we would not have otherwise. When Christ is the supreme love of a child, they desire to obey their parents and love their siblings. When Christ is the supreme love of a spouse, He compels them to love one another sacrificially as Christ has loved them. When Christ is the absolute love of a father or mother, that love produces in them an undying affection for their children.

Being a genuine disciple may mean losing a relationship with father or mother, brother or sister. It may mean a broken relationship with a best friend. Loving Christ might mean being disowned and rejected. Even so, Christ is worth it and much more. To follow Christ is to lay our families sacrificially on the altar, for Him to either remove or give back to us. If God sacrificed His own family for us, His Son, we should not be surprised if He asks the same of us.

Sacrifice of Time

Jesus won't be penciled into our schedules, He demands to command it. Jesus has made His requirements clear in John 12:25-26, "Whoever loves his life loses it, and whoever hates his life in this world will keep it for eternal life. If anyone serves me, he must follow me; and where I am, there will my servant be also. If anyone serves me, the Father will honor him." These verses should not be a defense for depression or cynicism. Jesus again is using an idiomatic phrase to express the point that no one can love their life more than Him and still be considered a true disciple.

John 12:25-26 is assaulting to the western individualistic personal planner. Planners, calendars, schedules, and GPS daily step counters all point to who a person is serving and what they truly value. Are the events, meetings, hangouts, phone calls, workouts, dinners out, and hobbies pointing to the life of a follower of Christ or the follower of fads, fashion, and fame? Let's make this even more personal.

If someone was to examine last week's schedule, from when you woke up to when you put your head on your pillow, what would they find? If they broke it down into a pie chart depicting categories for sleeping, meals eaten individually, movies, shopping, social media surfing, TV show watching, home renovation or landscaping, and such, what would the chart reveal about your pursuits? How would that chart compare with another chart of time in the word, with unbelievers or neighbors, serving the church, reading Christian books, praying for others, work that is glorifying God, serving others, and general thankfulness to God?

I made a pie chart recently for myself, and I was so sad by what I saw. I chose not to include sleep and mandatory working hours because it would throw everything off. So I calculated only hours I chose to use at my own discretion. To my shock, most of my discretionary time was primarily selfish or self-serving and formed a Pac Man shape with the mouth looking like it was slowly about to shut tight on something. The Pac Man self-serving time was eating my time with family, serving, and intentional focus on God's word.

Since then, Mark 10:45 has been convicting to me. Jesus says in this verse, "For even the Son of Man came not to be served but to serve, and to give his life as a ransom for many." If the Son of God came to serve sinners, then I should do the same. Our time is limited. The older I get the more precious I realized time is. Ephesians 5:15-16 says, "Look carefully then how you walk, not as unwise but as wise, making the best use of the time, because the days are evil."

If I live to increase my possessions or reputation on earth, I may gain the world, but I will lose Jesus. The true disciple must answer the question, *have I sacrificed my time to follow Jesus?*

Sacrifice of Money

Jesus wants to be both our joy and security. Money for many people puts Jesus in the octagon and tries to throw submission moves to get Jesus to tap. Perhaps, that is a crude way of saying it, but Jesus compared it with slavery or servanthood, so it isn't too far off. Jesus' statements on money are clear, "No one can serve two masters, for either he will hate the one and love the other, or he will be devoted to the one and despise the other. You cannot serve God and money" (Matt. 6:24). How people think of, strive after, and use money reveals what they value.

One of my absolute favorite things is seeing what happens in the workplace when the boss comes around. A high percentage of people immediately begin stepping on each other to try to please the boss. Why? Do they love this man or woman? Most likely not, but they realize what this person can do for them and their career, so they play nice. When money or the pursuit of money is the chief motivation it will always corrupt and distort people's actions. Someone can try to hide behind the mask of "improving quality of life", but often improvement means sacrificing opportunities for the gospel or straight-up disobeying commandments of Christ.

Most people will struggle with sacrificing money or wealth and the pursuit of it. The question is this, does your disciple's heartbeat infiltrate to how you view, think of, and use your money? Are you gradually bringing money up to Christ's sacrificial alter where you lay it before Him for His use and His pleasure? Be careful, this doesn't mean just giving more.

Simply giving more now than when you were first saved does not mean you have grown in generosity. Instead, you may just be making more than you have ever made, while the percentage given from your income is less than ever!

Too many Christians think that if they are giving 10% then money isn't a problem. You can give 90% and still have a problem with money. Jesus wants a complete holistic view of wealth that is uninformed by material possession. This doesn't mean you are not wise and diligent with what God has given you. To be sacrificial in worship with money is to release the thought that having more material, excess cash, an investment portfolio, or better quality of life will bring you any reward. Wealth is not the goal because your happiness and hope aren't rooted in it.

Is it sinful to be wealthy? Absolutely not. Is it wrong to have a Roth IRA? Nope. Is putting money aside for your children's college displaying a lack of faith? No. Saving and being wise with what God has blessed you with is good so that you can be a blessing to others. However, if that same wealth becomes your hope and security than it has taken the place of God. The disciple must analyze their habits with money prayerfully, asking God to show them how to balance sacrifice and prudence.

Context is king, and when the context surrounding Matthew 6:24 is examined, Jesus' words are made clear. Verses 19-21 say, "Do not lay up for yourselves treasures on earth, where moth and rust destroy and where thieves break in and steal, but lay up for yourselves treasures in heaven, where neither moth nor rust destroys and where thieves do not break in and steal. For where your treasure is, there your heart will be also." The true disciple seeks to sacrifice all desires of laying up treasure on earth because their heart belongs to Jesus.

Sacrifice of Comfortability

Jesus was the original creator of the phrase, "get comfortable being uncomfortable." Jesus demands what we don't naturally desire to give. Comfort. Yet, as with almost everything in the Christian life, when we sacrifice momentary worldly comforts, we are given a true all-encompassing comfort.

Think of the people Jesus has called and used greatly for His name. The disciples were constantly getting mocked, ridiculed, beaten, and thrown in jail. Not your typical Hollywoodized style pastors! Stephen was stoned to death, Peter ended up being crucified upside down, John exiled to the island of Patmos to die, and Paul killed in Rome. Those are just four examples. If we look at church history, full books have been written on the lives of the various martyrs of the faith.

I think the paradigm we see in the call of Paul isn't as unusual as many try to make it. Not many people were given visions of the risen Christ, but the reality behind Christ's call still stays the same. When Jesus calls him, he tells Ananias, "he is a chosen instrument of mine to carry my name before the Gentiles and kings and the children of Israel. For I will show him how much he *must suffer for the sake of my name*" (Acts 9:15-16). To follow Christ is to sacrifice relational, familial, physical, and financial comforts. But in doing so, we receive the greatest of comforts. Consider the following passage.

"Blessed be the God and Father of our Lord Jesus Christ, the Father of mercies and God of all **comfort**, who **comforts** us in all our affliction, so that we may be able to **comfort** those who are in any affliction, with the **comfort** with which we ourselves are **comforted** by God. For as we share abundantly in Christ's sufferings, so through Christ we share abundantly in **comfort** too. If we are afflicted, it is for your **comfort** and salvation; and if we are **comforted**, it is for your **comfort**, which you experience when you patiently endure the same sufferings that we suffer. Our hope for you is unshaken, for we know that as you share in our sufferings, you will also share in our **comfort**." - 2 Corinthians 1:3-7

The fundamental contradiction to the western mind is that suffering and affliction bring comfort. Paul is making a distinction between physical and spiritual comforts. Pain, suffering, and affliction in this life that is brought upon by faithfulness to Christ should only bring comfort. Why? Because it is evidence of your genuine conversion. Your suffering is making you more like Christ. Philippians 3:10, "that I may know him and the power of his resurrection, and may share his sufferings, becoming like him in his death, [11] that by any means possible I may attain the resurrection from the dead."

The true disciple desires to sacrifice momentary comforts to receive the comfort that calms, refreshes, and revives the soul. The comfort of Jesus Christ Himself.

Sacrifice of Prejudice

There are many forms of prejudice. Some are so subtle we don't even know we have them. Others are overt, communicated, and acted upon. The majority are somewhere on the spectrum in between. Prejudices can come from our upbringing, personal interactions, media coverage, and other experiences. For the disciple of Jesus, there is no other option but to kill our prejudice. Jesus requires that our bias, racism, elitism, and bigotry be brought to the altar to be slaughtered and scorched into ashes.

Governmentally, in our justice systems, we are to be righteous and fair. From the beginning, God has commanded this. Leviticus 19:15 says, "You shall do no injustice in court. You shall not be partial to the poor or defer to the great, but in righteousness shall you judge your neighbor." Wealth or status should have no bearing on one's case before the court. The same is true of race and cultural upbringing. As God extends the grace of Jesus Christ impartially to any who accept and believe, so we should be impartial in showing justice.

The church government is to lead with eyes purified by the gospel and not partiality. In 1 Timothy 5:21 Paul says, "In the presence of God and of Christ Jesus and of the elect angels I charge you to keep these rules without prejudging, doing nothing from partiality." This is immediately following a direct charge from Paul to the congregation and the elders. The congregation is not to bring false accusations against the elders and the elders are called to rebuke publicly those who persist in sin. Yet, this is to be done without thought to personal feelings of an individual. Disciples of Christ ought to encourage their church to rebuke sin, support godly leadership, and genuinely desire to see people meet Jesus. It is when we lose gospel focus that we begin to show partiality.

One senior pastor in the area where I worked was informed that his worship pastor was in deep personal sin against his family. Many men urged this senior pastor to confront this other staff member. However, the senior pastor's favoritism of his associate beat out his conviction to rebuke him, and he did nothing. The sad truth is this is common. Our prejudice for people's affections outweighs the severity of the promises of God. Romans 2:11, "For God shows no partiality."

Sacrifice of Rights

Lastly, we sacrifice our rights when we accept the sacrifice of Jesus. When I say rights, I am referring to those things we might think we naturally deserve.

Consider the American context. Every citizen is told from birth that they have certain inalienable rights. One of these is the right to pursue happiness. Regardless of how we intended this to be interpreted, it has a particularly complex meaning today. As I observe my fellow Americans, happiness is achieved by doing whatever will make the individual *feel* happy. Happiness is not a moral quality, it is an existential personal reality that is defined individually. It has no objective definition of achievement, only the emotional subjective feeling that someone receives once they have obtained it. But what makes us feel happy is not always what is permissible by God. It often is not.

This concept is what provoked Jonathan Edwards' discussion on the need for a change in our affections. The disciple surrenders their right to decide what brings them happiness. Once a disciple, our happiness is faithfulness. The rights we sacrifice might produce momentary sorrow, but will bring eternal delight.

What rights are disciples called to sacrifice?

Disciples are called to sacrifice rights for the sake of others. In 1 Corinthians 8, Paul addresses food that is sacrificed to idols. For some people in the Corinthian church, eating food sacrificed to idols was to participate in idolatry. For any Christian to partake appeared to them as participation in that pagan worship. Paul pointed out what other Christians were saying, that there is nothing evil inherently in the offered food. However, he ends with verse 12, "Therefore, if food makes my brother stumble, I will never eat meat, lest I make my brother stumble."

I love coffee. Love it. I enjoy the taste, the smell, the roasting process, and how beans from one climate can taste drastically different from beans in another.

At one of the churches I served at, there was a leader in the church who couldn't stand coffee and saw it as potentially a sinful addiction. I disagree obviously. I would love to tell you that I decided to never take a sip of coffee again lest I make my brother stumble. It would be awesome if I could say I went out of my way to make sure I showed favor to this brother and gave up my love for a well-roasted cup of coffee. In truth, while not intending to be vindictive, I did the opposite. I started a coffee ministry. I bought a commercial coffee machine and started pumping out six gallons of coffee per. The church drank every sip of it. Literally, there was never any left. And that is the definition of poor discipleship.

I thought the desires of others outweighed the convictions of one. But that is not the teaching of the Bible and Jesus. To follow Christ is to sacrifice things that we think we have a right to, both for His sake and the sake of those around us, so that we might encourage godly living.

Summary

Dietrich Bonhoeffer (1906-1945), was a pastor, theologian, spy, and martyr. Bonhoeffer was a respected intellect and theologian who earned the position of lecturer at the University of Berlin during the rise of Hitler in 1933. However, he refused to conform. Though on paper he was recruited by the infamous German secret service, he was serving as a double agent for the European alliance and assisting Jews in escaping Nazi control. He had an opportunity to escape the war and go stay in America as a lecturer, but he felt the call of God to return and share in the suffering of the Christians in Germany. In April of 1943, he was arrested and put into Tegel prison. In his final letters from prison, Dietrich Bonhoeffer wrote these words:

"To be a Christian does not mean to be religious in a particular way, to make something of oneself (a sinner, a penitent, or a saint) on the basis of some method or other, but to be a man—not a type of man, but the man that Christ creates in us. It is not the religious act that makes the Christian, but participation in the sufferings of God in the secular life."

Bonhoeffer had a simple and profound conviction. His life was bound to the will of God. He had an out. He had an opportunity to avoid the war, teach in a prestigious university, and maintain his position in the church. Instead, he chose to sacrifice. He chose to participate in the sufferings of Christ. Bonhoeffer had his eyes focused on eternity, which allowed him to see the present clearly.

A doctor, who witnessed Bonhoeffer's hanging one month before Germany's surrender, described the scene in the following manner:

"The prisoners ... were taken from their cells, and the verdicts of court martial read out to them. Through the half-open door in one room of the huts, I saw Pastor Bonhoeffer, before taking off his prison garb, kneeling on the floor praying fervently to his God. I was most deeply moved by the way this lovable man prayed, so devout and so certain that God heard his prayer. At the place of execution, he again said a prayer and then climbed the steps to the gallows, brave and composed. His death ensued in a few seconds. In the almost 50 years that I have worked as a doctor, I have hardly ever seen a man die so entirely submissive to the will of God."[xxiv]

The cross changes everything. Christ's sacrifice secures my salvation regardless of anything I do. And yet, his sacrifice demands that I too sacrifice. The heartbeat of a true disciple is to surrender things in their life keeping them from Jesus, obeying Jesus, or becoming more like Jesus. This involves sacrificing family, time, money, comfortability, prejudice, rights, and truly so much more. These are but a few categories that Jesus calls us to surrender in our walk with Him.

My challenge to you is to measure your heartbeat. Do you see a pulse of the gospel in your life? Is there real genuine heartfelt sacrifice for the sake of Jesus Christ? Can you write down tangible examples in your life? Would you sacrifice more just for the potential to know Christ better? What is stopping you from sacrificing? The disciple's heart must beat to surrender more and more to gain more and more of Jesus.

In the next chapter, we are going to see how sacrifice bleeds over into our willingness to surrender our sin and embrace the power of the Spirit to obey Christ.

Chapter 5: Obey

The Theological Significance of Obedience

"It is so hard to believe because it is so hard to obey." - Søren Kierkegaard

"Why?"

"Because I said so!"

When you read that simple transaction of words you may cringe, sigh, smile, or maybe think that is just how life goes. We are creatures who deal with obedience from birth. From the most developed intellectual societies to the most primitive, we instinctively obey something or someone. Call it submission, conformity, or oppression. Call it whatever you like. From birth, humanity is placed in a hierarchal relationship with the universe. You might call the laws natural or created, either way, we are under the law. We exist in a world of law, authority, and submission. Every person is forced to answer one basic question, "who will I obey?"

In the 1960s, Stanley Milgram conducted his famous scientific experiment on obedience and conformity.[xxv] He asked for general public volunteers to participate in what he told them was a study on memory. Essentially, participants were told they were in the role of the "Teacher" and were to instruct the "Learner" on their memory of particular words from previously recalled pairs. They were to administer increasing magnitude of electrical shocks if the "Learner" failed to remember the correct answer. What the volunteers did not know, was that the "Learner" was a part of the experiment and the shocks were not real. The point of the study was to see how far these random individuals would go with administering pain to their subjects.

The results were shocking. All participants willingly administered shocks of 300 volts with 65% going all the way to 450 volts. Even when the actor "Learner" screamed in pain most volunteers continued to administer higher levels of electric shocks. Why? There was another factor. An authority figure was present with them who was over the study. When the volunteer showed hesitation to administer the fake pain, the authority figure reminded them that this was part of the study and that they had to do it. They were instructed to prod the volunteer four times in increasing levels of intensity before allowing them to stop the study. This research compelled academics to conclude that the average person would kill a stranger if they were compelled by an insisting authority figure.

The baseline conclusion from basic observation and experimentation is that humanity has a natural propensity toward obedience. The question is what are you going to obey? Is it going to be Science, the Torah, the Koran, the Bible, Confucius, Scientology, Democracy, Republican, Democrat, Individualism, Socialism, Communism, or something else?

The topic of obedience is essential to what it means to be a disciple. In John 8:31-32 Jesus says, "if you abide in my word, you are truly my disciples, and you will know the truth and the truth will set you free." Only those who continue, remain, stay, and obey Jesus' word are those who are truly His disciples.

So, let's ask the question that every grubby cookie loving disobedient child asks. Why?

In this chapter, we will examine the theological significance of humanity's obedience. Starting with creation and ending with revelation we will examine what the scriptures say about our disposition to obedience, and why we venomously hate it.

Creation & Eden

Genesis 1:1, "In the beginning, God created the heavens and the earth." From its first words, scripture declares who is in the position of governance, authority, and power. God. Whatever comes next in this story, one thing is without question. Everything is subject to the sovereign power and rule of God. All things are born dependent upon God and subject to Him. The question is, will creation recognize His authority or not?

Genesis 1:26 & 28 says, "Let us make man in our image, after our likeness. And let them have dominion over the fish of the sea and over the birds of the heavens and over the livestock and over all the earth and over every creeping thing that creeps on the earth... 28. And God blessed them. And God said to them, "Be fruitful and multiply and fill the earth and subdue it, and have dominion..." God created humanity to be both in submission and in authority. He created us to be subject to Himself, but with the authority and responsibility for His creation. These verses are commonly known as the Creation Mandate. God declares that man is to have power over the earth to subdue it, cultivate it, and engage with it. We are both given orders and to give orders.

Stop for a moment and consider that childlike question, why are we called to obey? The reason is not all that satisfying at first. Elohim created humanity. Shall the created say to the creator I am greater than you? Will the created question the creator? Unless we deny the origin of humanity as depicted in the scriptures, we are left with no other alternative to submission. Our position, by design, is subjected to the character and person of God. To disregard Him is a distortion and perversion of our created nature. Thus, we obey because we were created to.

I was utterly amazed in the movie theatre while watching the film *Thor*. Marvel scripted one of the most fundamental theological truths known to humanity. When Loki makes his big reveal to earth, he gives a speech that causes people to cringe.

Loki, while wearing his reindeer antler crown thingy says, "Kneel...KNEEL! Is this not your natural state? It's the unspoken truth of humanity that you crave subjugation. The bright lure of freedom diminishes your life's joy in a mad scramble for power. For identity. You were made to be ruled. In the end, you will always kneel."

I lost my mind! Right there in Marvel's script, they nail it. The idea of autonomous hedonism, personal free discovery, or postmodernism are all lures that diminishes life's joy. Why? Because we were made to be ruled. But not by Loki. Not by Instagram and Facebook. But by God. We were made to be ruled by the all benevolent perfect life sustainer, our creator Himself.

Consider our created purposes in relation to sin. Sin is holistic disobedience. Sin is blatant insurgence against created purpose. Sin incorporates different levels of rebellion against God in heart, mind, and action. We already looked at Adam and Eve in chapter three but contemplate with me again their sin within the realm of obedience.

Adam and Eve were given one verbal rule, do not eat of the tree of knowledge of good and evil. When they decided together, after all Adam was right there next to Eve, to eat this fruit and disobey, several things happened.

First, they considered disobedience to provide a better reward than obedience. Essentially, their thoughts reflect a belief that it might be ***better*** for them to disobey God than to obey Him. This is the fundamental lie of Satan to all of humanity. Satan desires for every person to believe that disobeying God might be of benefit to them. Let's continue with the childish questioning. Why?

Satan tempts us to believe what he believes: God's way isn't the best way. Isaiah 14:13-14 says, "You said in your heart, I will ascend to heaven; above the stars of God, I will set my throne on high; I will sit on the mount of assembly in the far reaches of the north; I will ascend above the heights of the clouds; I will make myself like the Most High." The depiction of Babylon and Satan here are the same. The desire is to be God. To be the authority and power of the universe. For in Satan's mind, it is better for him to be in authority than to live under the authority of God. And he wants every one of God's creatures to share his belief.

Second, in their heart, they desired to have what God had forbidden. We have this still today. Anytime someone tells us we can't have something; it only increases our desire for that which we're told we can't have.

Experiment at home. Put a cookie jar on the counter and tell your children they can't have any cookies. They will just sit there and stare. They will begin to negotiate. Perhaps they will go off and play, but an hour or two later they will come back and ask if they can have one now that they have waited. Adam and Eve desired what they were told they could not have.

Lastly, their actions followed the decision of their mind and the desire of their heart. The fall did not start when they took the first bite. The sin started in their hearts and minds. It continued as Eve gazed upon the fruit and as Adam did nothing to stop her. It grew as Eve walked over and examined it, forcefully pulling it from its vine, and felt its features in the palm of her hand. The sin cemented as Adam watched his wife in the action of her disobedience, as he said nothing to stop her, and as he chose to follow her. Our sinful actions are simply the manifestations of the sins of heart and mind.

When we sin against God, we are holistically disobeying Him. We are desiring in our heart something other than Him. We are believing in our mind that His words are untrue. We are acting by our desire and belief which brings our fall.

The Fall and Following

Ever since the fall, we no longer are positive or even neutral in our inclinations toward obeying God. The heart of humanity changed. Whatever the status of humanity was initially in the garden, it has been altered. This change occurred once humanity was cursed and banished from the garden. But it starts first with the curse against Satan.

In his book, *God's Glory in Salvation through Judgement,* Dr. James Hamilton examines the intrinsic effect of the curse. Satan's temptation was nothing less than an assault on the goodness of God. For Satan, there is no hope or mercy shown. Dr. Hamilton clarifies this passage for us.

"The serpent will be in constant conflict with the woman and her seed. The word "seed" can refer to either the single or the collective seed of the woman. The serpent, agent of uncleanness who instigated transgression, will be ultimately defeated when the seed of the woman crushes his head. This points to the final defeat of evil, and it is here that salvation first comes through judgment."[xxvi]

The seed of the woman is a paradigm depiction of all the children of God. The culmination of the seed of the woman is the incarnate Christ who broke the chains of death through His perfect life, substitutionary death, and bodily resurrection. His work will be ultimately finished at His second coming. Satan is shown no mercy. Praise be to God the fate of humanity is different.

God chooses to be gracious to man. Instead of full

condemnation, there is mercy. The curse is still real. Because of their sin, Adam and Eve will experience struggle in marriage, pain in childbirth, and toil in work (Gen. 3:17-19). Then God does something strange. Genesis 3:21 says "And the Lord God made for Adam and for his wife garments of skins and clothed them." Death occurs. But not theirs. An animal's life sacrificed so Adam and Eve can be clothed. This first act of sacrificial death to clothe the unrighteousness of humanity is seen again at the cross with the offering being the Son of God.

To the dismay of Adam and Eve, their first child does not crush Satan. Nor does their next. Sadly, one crushes the other. The narrative of Genesis after the fall shows us that something has changed in the heart of man. Cain's descendant Lamech not only disobeys God, but he also finds pleasure and delight in doing so, boasting to his wives of the condemnation he brings upon himself. The story culminates in Genesis 6:5, "The Lord saw that the wickedness of man was great in the earth and that every intention of the thoughts of his heart was only evil continually." Something changed. Humanity not only had a disposition to disobey God but delighted in doing so.

The flood narrative is incredibly purposeful. Genesis 6:8-9 reads, "But Noah found favor in the eyes of the Lord... Noah was a righteous man, blameless in his generation." The proclivity of an unengaged reader is to assume Noah was spared because he was righteous and therefore desired to please God. On the contrary, God's favor upon Noah enabled him to desire to please and obey God.

The word "favor" is the Hebrew word for grace. It is and always will be God's grace that enables a person to desire to obey Him. The flood narrative shows us that humanity does not have an outward problem, but rather inward. For even after all the destruction and display of God's wrath, Noah ends up getting drunk and Ham uncovering his nakedness. Whatever this means, we know it is abominable. Later, Ham ends up fathering one of the most wicked nations, the Canaanites.

All this to say, the problem of humanity stems from the internal desires of the heart. Our desire is not to obey God. Our natural inclination is to reject His reign and rule. Without God's grace, humanity is lost.

Grace of the Law

The law is God's grace to Israel and all humanity because it displays our true desires and desperate need for God's intervention. From the institution of the law to the cross of Christ, we see the utter depravity of man and our desperate need for God's grace.

Before God came to Moses, he came to Abraham. He revealed Himself to then Abram, a pagan and likely moon worshiper. In Genesis 12:1-3, God promises to make Abraham into a great people, give him a great land, and through him bring about a great blessing. Childless, Abraham is baffled how God will do this. In Genesis15:5-6, God takes Abram out of his tent and gives him the most amazing promise. He says to him, "And he brought him outside and said, "Look toward heaven, and number the stars, if you are able to number them." Then he said to him, "So shall be your offspring." And Abram believed the Lord, and he counted it to him as righteousness.

God comes to this pagan who has no desire to obey God and shows him grace. He makes him an unconditional promise. God will do these things for Abraham regardless of what Abraham does.

The result of God's grace is our affections change.

Abraham begins to obey God. He begins to desire to obey God.

His faith so increases, that he is willing to kill his miracle child Isaac, simply because God instructed him to do so. Without the grace of God acting in our life, we will always determine to disregard Him. The best illustrator of this fact is the law.

The law that God gives to Israel on Mt. Sinai is a significant act of perfect grace. Exodus 19:5-6 says, "Now, therefore, if you will indeed obey my voice and keep my covenant, you shall be my treasured possession among all peoples, for all the earth is mine; and you shall be to me a kingdom of priests and a holy nation."

The purpose of the law is perfect.

The law provides both godly direction and a way to expel ungodly behavior. The purpose was to show man his sin and utter need for God's grace. Sin tainted everyone. Even the high priest had to cleanse himself before he could do anything on behalf of the people. The law was meant to point toward God's providential grace in providing a substitute for sin. But instead, Israel made the law into God. The law became a standard for righteousness rather than a sign pointing to our sinfulness.

I remember the first week of summer break when I decided to visit my family doctor. I was between my sophomore and junior year at the Moody Bible Institute in Chicago. During that sophomore year, I had completed 36 credits, worked three jobs, volunteered as a youth pastor, and attempted to have a dating relationship. When my doctor took my blood pressure it showed I was around 153/92 mmHg. This machine said I was in the first stage of hypertension. In short, something was wrong, and I needed an immediate course correct as a 20-year-old.

This is the law. It is diagnostic of the heart. It reveals a condition that needs correcting. But all it can do is point to correction, it cannot fix the problem and it was never designed too. God perfectly created the law to point back to our need for His grace and our complete reliance upon Him.

Paul takes up this conversation in his letter to the Galatians. In 3:23-24 he says, "Now before faith came, we were held captive under the law, imprisoned until the coming faith would be revealed. So then, the law was our guardian until Christ came, so that we might be justified by faith." When he wrote to the Romans he says in 3:19-20, "Now we know that whatever the law says it speaks to those who are under the law, so that every mouth may be stopped, and the whole world may be held accountable to God. For by the works of the law no human being will be justified in His sight, since through the law comes knowledge of sin." The law is given so that we can see how our desires and affections are contrary to God's. When given the choice between God glorifying or self-serving action, we will always choose the latter that glorifies and satisfies ourselves.

Don't miss that. Our natural inclination is to glorify and satisfy our self.

I find it interesting that non-Christians tend to embrace this truth whereas professing Christians are resistant. While writing this chapter I am deployed to the Middle East. Many of my military brothers in arms are not Christians. Yet, when I bring up the nature of humanity, most of them quickly agree. Most of the older guys in the group have seen the earlier stages of the War in Iraq and Afghanistan. Through their traveling and personal experience, they readily agree with the scripture's assessment of the condition of man.

Paul comments on several Psalms that illustrate this point. He says in Romans 3:10-18, "None is righteous, no not one; no one seeks God. All have turned aside; together they have become worthless; no one does good, not even one... There is no fear of

God before their eyes."

He concludes in Romans 3:23, "For all have sinned and fall short of the glory of God." No one can be saved by the law or any other independent means because ultimately our desires are distorted. When Paul writes to the Ephesians, he says, "For by grace you have been saved through faith. And this is not of your own doing; it is the gift of God, not a result of works, so that no one may boast." No one can please God apart from God's grace allowing it.

Apart from God's grace, we cannot do good.

I know that seems like a significant generalization. But if you consider the word good as defined by God rather than our perceptions it proves true. The only way our words, actions, and thoughts are considered good before God is when we are transformed by and united to Christ.

Grace of the Cross

Entire volumes are written on the grace we have received from Jesus. Here I want to highlight the grace that comes from His perfect obedient life and death.

I was driving back from a training operation with a Catholic friend of mine. As we were weaving between mo-ped drivers along an Asian island coast, our conversation turned toward the humanity of Christ.

"He was a real guy! He probably looked at girls, swore on accident, told a lie, and drank a little too much on occasion." He said with at least partial conviction.

I asked him the following question, "then who paid the price for His sin?"

Silence.

Jesus' perfect obedience forever changed our ability to obey. 2 Corinthians 5:21 says, "For our sake he made him to be sin who knew no sin, so that in him we might become the righteousness of God."

Remember the law, before the priests could administer sacrifices for others, they had to do it first for themselves. Jesus requires no sacrifice because He lived perfectly. As the eternal Son, He can substitute Himself for our eternal debt.

As a result, when we believe in Him, we are united to Him. In Galatians 2:20, Paul is adamant, "I have been crucified with Christ. It is no longer I who live, but Christ who lives in me." When Jesus talks to the disciples in the upper room He says, "If anyone loves me, he will keep my word, and my Father will love him, and we will come to him and make our home with him" (John 14:23). Michael Horton writes, "The righteousness of God is a command that condemns us all, but the righteousness from God is a gift that saves all who believe."[xxvii] Our union to Christ provides us will the ability to listen, understand, follow, and obey.

Jesus says in John 15:5 "I am the vine; you are the branches. Whoever abides in me and I in him, he it is that bears much fruit, for apart from me you can do nothing." Unless we are united to Christ, we can do nothing. When we are united to Him, through the indwelling power of the Spirit, we can obey!

Summary

When Janelle and I had our first daughter I was amazed by the helplessness of this little girl. The poor child had no way to feed herself, change herself, move herself, or communicate what she needed. The only possible function that this beautiful baby girl could do is scream. And scream she did. She would scream like her life depended on it. To her credit, in her mind, it probably did. She could do nothing. Without the aid of someone else, she was hopeless. That is our position before God apart from grace. We have only one option. Beg, scream, cry out in utter desperation and submission to God for His grace like our lives depend on it. Because they do.

The answer to the why is somewhat simple. *I obey because I was created too.*

The answer to the how is equally simple. *I can obey because He enables me too.*

The reason why we don't often obey is more complex.

Depravity makes our created purpose an impossible reality apart from grace. The only way we can fulfill our created purpose and obey God is through our union to His perfectly obedient Son, Jesus. His banishment to a cross brings about our freedom from sin and our ability to obey.

In this next chapter, we will look at the specifics of God's varied grace and how true disciples evidence union to Christ through obedience.

Chapter 6: Obey

A true Disciple will Obey

"Disobedience is the true foundation of liberty. The obedient must be slaves." - Henry David Thoreau

Do you find yourself agreeing or disagreeing with Thoreau?

I suppose it depends on your vantage point. Perhaps your immediate propensity is to consider the mundane ignorance of social conformity. Thereby, you judge Thoreau correct. People who blindly obey the noise of culture shift, without critical thought or judgment, are slaves to trends and mere opinion of the masses. Slavery in your mind is likely defined by entrapment to thoughtlessness without hope, desire, or possibility of escape. Or maybe, you agree simply because to only obey without question, objection, and/or resistance seems robotic, inhumane, and unprogressive.

One of the most prominent modern atheists wrote about a professor of his. The professor dedicated his life to the study of a metabolic synthesis. While making his presentation on what was widely agreed upon as fact, a student interrupted with a question. His question exposed an error in the professor's research that in and of itself discredited 10 years of his work. Instead of fighting in defense of his research, the professor took a long thoughtful pause. He then did something extraordinary. He applauded the young man and thanked him for his contribution to modern science.

At that moment, it appeared that disobedience, in the sense of non-conformity to an authority figure and renowned scientist, actually demonstrated progressive liberty. The atheist also used this story in comparison to the perceived unquestionable, illogical, blindly followed Christian faith.

Thoreau's statement and this atheist's perspective are provoking because they hinge on the subjective. Disobedience to what? To an assumed scientific theory? To government? To parental authority? What is the object that is being disobeyed or obeyed? For if the object being obeyed is false, or has even a chance of falsehood, then Thoreau's statement stands true with regards to absolute obedience. However, if the object is found to always be true, then the statement is found false or at least deceptive. Everything hinges on truth.

Unquestionable obedience can only stand on a foundation of irrefutable truth. Only one person claims to not only have the truth, but that He is the truth. John 14:6 "I am the way, and the truth, and the life. No one comes to the Father except through me."

Jesus is explicit, a true disciple will obey God's word. The central passage for understanding this is John 8:31-32, "If you abide in my word, you are truly my disciples, and you will know the truth, and the truth will set you free." Jesus disagrees with Thoreau, for only in obedience can you experience true liberty. A genuine disciple will continually seek to obey God. This is not to say a true disciple no longer struggles with sin. Rather, as a true disciple is sanctified, they will continually rest and seek after the grace of God in their everyday life.

This chapter will focus on how God's grace elects, frees, informs, empowers, and sustains the disciple's heart. As the disciple receives a regenerated heart by God's grace, they are equally sanctified by grace. God's grace will forever alter a disciple's affections and enables them to obey the words of God.

God's Grace in Election:

Grace is best defined as unmerited divine favor. As we saw in the last chapter, no one is righteous. No one deserves God or eternal life with Him in heaven. Every person lacks what is necessary to enter His holy presence, which is perfection (Matt. 5:48). Thus, as God has always done with His people, He graciously chooses those who are truly His.

I assume that your blood pressure just began to spike. Calvinists are saying, "finally! Election! I have been waiting for this the entire book! Living for Jesus is great and all, but election is true Christianity!"

The Arminian leaning individuals are like, "great another guy who cares more about 16th century dead people than currently living lost people." Right now, Arminians are considering tossing this book into the kitchen garbage can, while the Calvinists are getting ready to share it on Facebook.

Cards on the table, I am a Calvinist. I say that with the understanding that both Arminian and Calvinist brothers and sisters have preconceived notions of what that means and are likely both misled. Regardless, it is impossible for a human to believe in God apart from God's grace. This grace is manifested in His predetermined election in His Son Jesus Christ. Believe it or not, both Jacob Arminius and John Calvin believed this. They simply disagreed about what election looks like in time and in the will of the believer.[xxviii] The reason they both agreed is that the Bible doesn't leave room for disagreement on the reality of election. Every Christian has been graciously elected by God before the world began.

The letter to the Ephesians proves the majority of what both Calvin, Arminius, and Christians in all centuries have believed. People cannot be saved apart from the grace of God. Paul wrote this letter extremely intentionally. After all, it is inspired by the Spirit!

The first half is our identity, and the second half outlines actions that flow from it. The explanation of sinner to saint starts with predetermined grace-filled election.

Ephesians 1:3-6 says, "Blessed be the God and Father of our Lord Jesus Christ, who has blessed us in Christ with every spiritual blessing in the heavenly places, even as *he chose us in him before the foundation of the world*, that we should be holy and blameless before him. *In love he predestined us* for adoption to himself as sons through Jesus Christ, according to the purpose of His will, to the praise of His glorious grace, with which he has blessed us in the Beloved."

To be a Christian is to be chosen by God. A person can reason this truth in different ways, but the core truth that God has chosen us to be in Christ remains. The idea of being "in Christ" is a book in and of itself. But one thing it surely means is to conform our wills to His will, thereby, our actions to His actions. God's gracious election enables our true obedience, for without it we would be hopeless.

Ephesians 2:1-10 says, "And you were dead in the trespasses and sins in which you once walked, following the course of this world, following the prince of the power of the air, the spirit that is now at work in the sons of disobedience— among whom we all once lived in the passions of our flesh, carrying out the desires of the body and the mind, and were by nature children of wrath, like the rest of mankind. *But God*, being rich in mercy, because of the great love with which he loved us, even when we were dead in our trespasses, made us alive together with Christ—by grace you have been saved— and raised us up with him and seated us with him in the heavenly places in Christ Jesus, so that in the coming ages he might show the immeasurable riches of his grace in kindness toward us in Christ Jesus. For by grace you have been saved through faith. And this is not your own doing; it is the gift of God, not a result of works, so that no one may boast. For we are his workmanship, created in

Christ Jesus for good works, which God prepared beforehand, that we should walk in them."

To be a Christian is to be chosen by God, to be freed from sin, and to be created anew in Christ for good works foreordained by God. Before Christ we were spiritually dead, following our natural desires to disobey God. But God. Those two words represent the love and predetermined plan of redemption. And His plan included us even when we were in the darkest trenches of our sin.

God's grace in election humbles and emboldens the disciple! Life ebbs and flows between feelings of righteousness and sinfulness. God's gracious election humbles us when we are tempted to think we are doing well. Similarly, it emboldens us when we are in the shame of our own sinfulness. For He has forgiven our past, present, and future sin. Therefore, the disciple should display a humble confidence to proclaim and walk in the grace of God's election.

At the same time, we cannot cheapen God's grace. Dietrich Bonheoffer says it best, "Cheap grace is preaching forgiveness without requiring repentance, baptism without church discipline, Communion without confession.... Cheap grace is grace without discipleship, grace without the cross, grace without Jesus Christ, living and incarnate."[xxix] When we allow disobedience in ourselves or other disciples go unchecked, we cheapen grace.

Disobedience is sin and is counter to the new nature of a Christian. Perhaps like Thoreau, you consider this demand for obedience to be slavery. Paul would agree with you. In almost every letter he introduces himself as a slave of Christ Jesus. Obedience to Christ is slavery. But only in Christ-centered slavery is there true genuine liberty.

God's Grace Delivers Freedom

Freedom is not properly defined in and of itself. Freedom requires an antagonist or circumstance for it to be rightly understood. Imagine if you walked into a Starbucks at 7 am when the frantic coffee rush is at its peak, and yelled at the top of your lungs, "I am free!!!" Besides the awkward silence or potential jokester's response, I imagine someone might say, "Cool bro, free from what?" Freedom is only rightly understood when it is examined in the context of a previous existence.

When I was in high school my best friend Austin and I would use the word freedom in a different sense. Whenever one of us ended a relationship, or what we thought was a relationship with a girl, we would call out like William Wallace "Freedom!" Of course, this was a desperate attempt at false masculinity, however, we had fun with it. Our freedom was defined by a previous existence compared to a present circumstance.

Consider today's pinnacle representation of freedom, America. This country has bled and sacrificed unimaginable pains to say that it is free. However, along with our claim to freedom, we have an interesting tag line that appears every Memorial Day and Independence Day. The line reads, "Freedom isn't free." Many men and women have suffered, sacrificed, and died for this freedom.

What then does freedom mean? It is defined by years of pain and suffering. In the beginning, it meant freedom from taxation without representation. It then moved toward freedom by legislation. It continued by giving certain unalienable rights to its citizens. But then who would determine citizenship? There was still oppression since not everyone agreed about who deserved these rights. Wars were fought abroad and at home to define who we are as humans, and what we truly believed is within the rights of the individual. We are still fighting this fight today. By pain, sweat, blood, and death we are still defining what it means to be free.

The Christian understanding of freedom is similar but different. John 8:31-32 "So Jesus said to the Jews who had believed him, If you abide in my word, you are truly my disciples, and you will know the truth, and the truth will set you free." We have been set free from Satan, sin, and death by faith in the perfect life, death, and resurrection of Christ. Galatians 5:16 says, "But I say, walk by the Spirit, and you will not gratify the desires of the flesh." We can conquer sin. Yet, like Paul, "I do not understand my own actions. For I do not do what I want, but I do the very thing I hate" (Romans 7:15).

Additionally, Christian freedom is explained in the context of our previous existence apart from Christ. But unlike America, we have the complete definition. Freedom is separation from sin and union to Christ. Apart from Christ, we could not achieve obedience. As Romans 3 discusses, no one is good or desires to please God. But by God's election, in Christ's sacrifice and death, we are given a new nature that has enabled us by the Holy Spirit, to obey God in action and heart desire.

Galatians 2:20 says, "I have been crucified with Christ. It is no longer I who live, but Christ who lives in me. And the life I now live in the flesh I live by faith in the Son of God, who loved me and gave himself for me." The believer is united to Christ through the indwelling of the Holy Spirit. Jesus promised this before His death. John 14:23, "If anyone loves me, he will keep my word, and my Father will love him, and we will come to him and make our home with him."

The Father and Son make their home in the believer through the indwelling of the Holy Spirit. In His death, Jesus freed sinners from their sin nature, and gave them a new nature to obey God by the Holy Spirit. Therefore, one unmistakable sign of genuine belief in Jesus Christ is real heartfelt obedience to Christ.

A friend of mine is convinced he is a born-again Christian. He believes with certainty that when he dies he will see Saint Peter at the gates of Heaven, and Peter will gesture to him to walk through the gates while saying, "well done good and faithful servant." This same friend sees absolutely no problem with his past and current history of multiple ongoing affairs. In his mind, Jesus has forgiven him based upon his confession of his belief in Jesus' resurrection and lordship. Is my friend a true disciple of Jesus? His actions state his position. While he may have genuine belief, James tells us, even the demons believe and shutter (James 2:19). When a disciple receives the grace of God to become a disciple of Jesus, they not only receive that ability to be free from sin, they also desire freedom from it.

God's Grace Enables Genuine Obedience

We have seen in scripture that we are dead in our sin apart from Christ. But because of God's gracious election and Christ's sacrificial death and resurrection, we are given eyes to believe and receive freedom from the bondage to sin. In short, because of God's grace, we can obey.

What does this mean? It means every daily act of obedience is the result of the grace of God. Regardless of the Arminian or Calvinist perspective, God's gracious election enables our obedience to Christ.

Therefore, every act of obedience to God is an expression of the grace of God in the disciple's life.

Notice what is completely void from my explanation. Never does action earn status before God. No work is ever said to improve a person's position before God except the work of Jesus. You might say, well didn't Abraham believe and it was credited to him as righteousness? Yes! This is what Paul mentions in Romans 4 as evidence to God's election that enabled Abraham's faith. Faith, belief, and genuine trust in God are dependent upon God's first action upon us. Consider the simple verse in 1 John 4:19, "We love because he first loved us." Every pure action and holy word that we utter is a result of God's graciousness to us.

*Obedience assists in **proving** a true disciple of Christ, but does not **make** a disciple of Christ.*

Christianity is wrestling today over this topic of obedience. Is it essential? Can I knowingly and willfully disobey God and be a Christian? Do I have to attend "Church" to be a Christian? How much do I have to obey to be considered good? God cares about the heart and not about actions, right?

I am writing this chapter on Christmas day overseas while on a deployment. Here, teammates and coworkers continue to ask the same types of questions like, "how much sin can I do and still be saved?" Or, "how much bad can I do while saying I am a Christian and still be forgiven?" I have been asked, "Can I maintain my sexually involved relationship with my girlfriend and still be a Christian?" Multiple people have said, "I believe in Jesus, but not organized religion, therefore I don't go to church." However, on the opposite spectrum, when I was a pastor, I used to get asked often, "how much do I need to obey in order to be saved?" People in the church asked, "If I am at church every Sunday, read my bible and pray with my family, provide charity, and live respectfully to others, is that enough?" I remember one individual stating, "I am saved because I have been baptized and confessed my sin."

Though they may appear to be opposite, these questions and statements are really very similar. Both sides are trying to discuss salvation as if it is up to the individual to attain or lose. They are trying to understand and grasp salvation outside of being a disciple of Jesus.

The Apostle John wrote the letter 1 John to clarify these types of questions and statements. His conclusion is if someone is walking in continual disobedience, that person is proving by their actions that they do not believe. 1 John 3:6-7 says, "No one who abides in him keeps on sinning; no one who keeps on sinning has either seen him or known him. Little children, let no one deceive you. Whoever practices righteousness is righteous, as he is righteous." His point is modest. The true disciple's affections shift from desiring sin to desiring holiness.

Obedience or disobedience does nothing for your salvation except provide evidence of its reality or absence.

Today I chose to go to a church service. I chose to sing in front of my friends who think singing is silly. I chose to pray in front of others. I chose to publicly participate in communion. I chose to be potentially belittled by others for my faith. I chose to do these things. I chose to do them because I believe obedience to God is better than following my disobedient impulses. I have undergone a change of affections. However, never would I be inclined to do these things if God hadn't changed my heart. Therefore, His grace generates my obedience and His praise.

When examined through the lens of grace, obedience is the result of an overwhelmed heart. Many well-intentioned confessing people live their life by a set of dutiful rules. They must go to church, pray, read their bible, give their money, not cuss, not watch R-rated movies, no sex outside of marriage, no impure thoughts, no alcohol, modest clothing, honesty, hard work ethic, and the list goes on and on. The result is thousands of people feeling like they just need to "be better." They say things like, I need to read more, I need to pray more, I need to stop having bad thoughts, I need to give more, I need to work on patience, I need to forgive people, I need to stop being so angry, I need to love my spouse better, I need to love my kids better, I need to trust God more.

WHY?!

That is what I want to scream whenever I hear someone saying these things. Why do they *need* to be better? The only reason I can think of, is that they are convinced their relationship with God is determined upon what they dos. This reveals a heart that does not understand grace.

The discipleship relationship centers on grace resulting in an inclination shift toward obedience. No longer is obedience a box to be checked but a delight they are enabled to walk in. How can they not forgive when they have been so forgiven? How can they be anything other than faithful to their spouse as Christ is ever faithful to them? How can they not speak with kindness when He speaks to them with kindness? Obedience is the only proper response to grace. And it is the natural response that true disciples will display.

You are probably thinking then, is there no effort in obedience? If someone puts forth the effort to obey, does that then make them a legalist who is trying to earn and attain their position before God? As Paul would say, by no means!

God's Grace Empowers and Informs Effort

What compels personal effort to pursue righteousness? Every Christian will put forth considerable effort to resist sin and obey Jesus. The difference between legalistic effort and grace centered effort is a matter of theological perspective that leads to genuine heartfelt motivation.

Right belief produces right motivation, which enables right action.

Think of our theological perspective as a world view. It is the glasses by which we look to interpret our world around us. How we think about time, culture, money, music, romance, religious practice, family, enemies, friends, everything and anything. When our theological perspective is clear, defined, and saturated with God's gracious biblical truths, it produces a desire to put forth effort out of gratitude rather than obligation. As the mind understands and believes more of God's truth, genuine heartfelt motivation arises. This motivation comes from love, not law. It comes from grace, not self. It cannot be ignored nor suppressed. Grace-centered theological perspective produces heartfelt motivation, that results in the exertion of human effort, not out of duty, but desire.

Consider prayer. Unmerited divine favor in election empowers a heart of profound prayer. Thankfulness considering our unworthiness. Petition on behalf of those whose hearts only God can change. Praise for any and every good work we can do, because of our freedom in Christ. Through the Spirit, we can pray with groanings too deep for words. Prayer is also adoration for God's patience with a sinful people. Prayers that are not focused merely upon health or wealth but matters of the soul. Grace-centered theological perspective not only empowers prayer, but it also enhances it and reveals it as essential to daily life. We could say this of all spiritual disciplines.

The problem is we often don't take time to put on our glasses. Imagine you are one of the many severely visually impaired people in our society who require glasses to see either near or far away. If you leave the house for a full workday without your glasses or contacts, you are in for a world of hurt! After a full day of squinting and seeing blurry images you will be frustrated by your absentmindedness and have a raging headache.

In our busyness, we forget grace-centered theological perspective. The result is our heartfelt motivation dissipates and obedience becomes a chore rather than a joy. Like a person without their glasses, we are frustrated because we are not seeing clearly.

When a true disciple keeps their theological perspective, they cannot contain their heartfelt motivation for Christ. They will put forth exceeding amounts of effort, not because of mere duty, but because of pure love. This is what Jonathan Edwards seeks to explain in *A Treatise Concerning Religious Affections*. In his introduction he asks, "what is the nature of true religion?"[xxx] True religion, according to Edwards, will manifest itself in certain signs of religious affections. These affections Edwards describes as, "no other than the more vigorous and sensible exercises of the inclination and will of the soul."[xxxi] In my reasoning, effort and Edward's "vigorous and sensible exercises" are synonymous. Edwards first discusses twelve signs that are uncertain of genuine faith, followed by twelve that are certain. All twelve genuine signs of sincere discipleship are smothered with overwhelming affection and adoration for the divine and His Word. A disciple will exercise vigorous effort to obey Jesus, but not because they have to, because they actually want to!

Grace-centered theological perspective leads naturally to heartfelt motivation that puts forth effort to worship God, even in difficulty.

Horatio Spafford is a perfect example.[xxxii] Spafford wrote the classic hymn "It is Well." Spafford had lost his son at age four, to scarlet fever. Two years later he, his wife, and four daughters, Annie, Maggie, Bessie, and two-year-old Tanetta, decided to travel to England to accompany the preacher D. L. Moody. Business detained Spafford, but he sent his family ahead of him. He received word that the ship *Ville du Havre* had sunk, and survivors were unknown.

Shortly thereafter, he received a telegram with two words. It was from his wife. It read, "saved alone." All four of his daughters perished in the wreck. He wrote this famous hymn after these events. The first verse says, "when peace, like a river, attendeth my way, when sorrows like sea billows roll; whatever my lot, thou hast taught me to say, it is well, it is well with my soul." To write these words, let alone sing them, requires not only a powerful theological perspective, but grace empowered emotions. Spafford experienced sorrows as great as rolling sea billows. However, he did not run from his emotions. He embraced them with the grace of God and chose to allow his grief to become worship. This type of maximal effort to worship and trust in God can only be explained by grace.

Spafford's theological perspective births a heartfelt motivation to worship amidst exceeding grief. But what about when I am not grieving? What about when things are going well? The same theological perspective and heartfelt motivational effort that Spafford used to work through a time of grief, should also guide us in times of success.

Have you noticed that the hardest times to pray, spend time in the word, give generously, and think of the needs of others is when life is going well? Why is it that when tragedy strikes people pray? Why is it that when the bank account is low or empty, people show up at church? Why is it that when someone is ill or dies, people call out to God? Why does it take a rebellious child for a parent to open their Bibles? The reason is people become confident in their abilities and forget about grace. They lose theological perspective and their heartfelt motivation. They turn from grace-centered effort to self-driven ability.

Israel is a prime example. Israel was delivered from Egypt, provided for and sustained in the desert, and given military victory to secure the promised land. They begin with worshipping the Lord for fulfilling His promise to them. Then they divide up the land and begin to settle. Homes are built. Gardens are planted. Territories and city lines established. Marriages occur and children are born. Slowly, they begin to forget the one who delivered, sustained, and fought for them.

"And the people of Israel did what was evil in the sight of the Lord and served the Baals... Everyone did what was right in his own eyes" (Judges 2:11 and 21:25).

This is the state of many American and Christian communities all over the world. They have abandoned their theological perspective and heartfelt motivation to do what seems right in their own eyes. Their effort is empowered and informed by an ever-changing culture, not the changeless sovereign God and His inerrant word. True discipleship of Christ is a reliance upon grace to fuel the maximal effort to obey God in every area of life, regardless of present circumstances.

Every true disciple ought to work with extreme effort to obey God in their life. Effort produced and informed by the knowledge and power of God's grace.

God's Grace Sustains our Discipleship

All this grace talk is great, but what happens when we disobey as a genuine disciple? Does disobedience discredit our faith? I remember during my undergraduate, I was eating lunch with the soon to be best man at my wedding. We were deep into a disagreement about obedience. The premise that was in discussion was this statement, "every act of disobedience is a result of disbelief." I adamantly denied it at first. However, I now see no alternative but accepting it now.

Sin is any form of disobedience to God. It can be breaking His natural, moral, or written law. When we sin, we call God a liar. For He has declared that His direction is not only required, but also the best for us. However, when we deviate from His direction, we are saying that there is something better for us then what He has given or directed. Thus, sin is disbelief in God. Disobedience is a result of disbelief.

But how can a person be a believer and at the same time disbelieve God? Doesn't that disbelief negate any claim to belief? Those two questions were my initial reaction. Consider the following scriptures:

James 2:19 "You believe that God is one; you do well. Even the demons believe—and shudder."

John 2:23-25 "Now when he was in Jerusalem at the Passover Feast, many believed in his name when they saw the signs that he was doing. But Jesus on his part did not entrust himself to them, because he knew all people and needed no one to bear witness about man, for he himself knew what was in man."

John 6:66 "After this many of his disciples turned back and no longer walked with him."

Mark 9:24 "Immediately the father of the child cried out and said, "I believe; help my unbelief!"

Psalm 32:1-2 "Blessed is the one whose transgression is forgiven, whose sin is covered. Blessed is the man against whom the LORD counts no iniquity, and in whose spirit there is no deceit."

Romans 4:1-5 "What then shall we say was gained by Abraham, our forefather according to the flesh? For if Abraham was justified by works, he has something to boast about, but not before God. For what does the Scripture say? "Abraham believed God, and it was counted to him as righteousness." Now to the one who works, his wages are not counted as a gift but as his due. And to the one who does not work but believes in him who justifies the ungodly, his faith is counted as righteousness."

James 2:19, John 2:23-25 and 6:66 all show belief that does not lead to salvation. Yet, Mark 9:29 shows a conflicting belief. A desperate father who recognizes his lack of belief, but also confesses some form of belief. Psalm 32 and Romans 4 assists with the understanding that God graciously sustains true belief by overlooking iniquity and considering one righteous regardless of action. What does this then mean with regards to disobedience as a Christian?

If the result of disbelief is disobedience, then God's grace must sustain true believers in times of disbelief.

The church, over the years, has labeled this concept as eternal security, perseverance of the saints, or the idea of "once saved always saved." Salvation is God's grace given to those who truly believe. Thus, when we fall into unbelief and sin, we should be condemned again because at that moment we are not believing in God. But God's grace is greater than our disbelief.

Romans 8:1-4 "There is therefore now no condemnation for those who are in Christ Jesus. For the law of the Spirit of life has set you free in Christ Jesus from the law of sin and death. For God has done what the law, weakened by the flesh, could not do. By sending His own Son in the likeness of sinful flesh and for sin, he condemned sin in the flesh, in order that the righteous requirement of the law might be fulfilled in us, who walk not according to the flesh but according to the Spirit."

There is no condemnation in Christ. The Holy Spirit has sealed us for the day of deliverance. We are sheep protected in the fold of God, watched always by our shepherd who keeps all out who would deceive, and keeps all in who are tempted to wander.

God's grace sustains genuine disciples of Christ. He does this through the Holy Spirit in a profound way. For true believers, *every act of disobedience and disbelief is an opportunity to obey and demonstrate belief.* I know. This seems completely contradictory. But consider with me how God's grace sustains us in disbelief.

I like money. I enjoy having and spending money. One of my challenges is giving generously. I know scripture calls me to it, and yet, I often find myself disobeying God's call on my heart to give. Every time I disobey, I can feel the guilt, the pressing of the Spirit convicting my heart, instructing me on what I need to do. The Spirit takes my disbelief and presents me with an opportunity to obey God and practice belief.

God has made it clear what we are to do when we sin. 1 John 1:9 says, "If we confess our sins, he is faithful and just to forgive us our sins and to cleanse us from all unrighteousness." When we confess our sin, we practice obedience to God's word and demonstrate genuine belief. Galatians 5:16 says to "walk by the Spirit, and you will not gratify the desires of the flesh." After I confess, I must follow the leading of the Spirit who will guide me into godly action.

For me, to obey during disobedience looks like this. I recognize by the conviction of the Holy Spirit that I have sinned by being greedy with my money. By the grace of God, I confess that greed as sin and disbelief in His word. I then praise Him for His grace in already forgiving me in Jesus Christ and not counting this iniquity over me. I ask for cleansing from this sin and that I would trust in Christ to obey. By the leading of the Spirit, I then will seek to obey by demonstrating generosity in both action and heart. Once both action and heart have aligned to the leading of the Spirit, I return in prayer. My focus is to praise God for allowing me to both obey His word and demonstrate His gracious gift of genuine belief in Him.

This is the sanctification process. God's grace sustains the disciple in spiritual security and continually cleanses the disciple throughout their life, making them holy.

Summary

A true disciple will obey by the grace of God. They also will recognize that obedience does not earn their discipleship, but rather assists in proving it. Obedience is made possible by God's gracious election. He enables us to believe and be set free from the bondage of sin. By His grace and indwelling of the Spirit, we can please Him and obey His commands. But obedience is not something to be checked off a to-do list. Obedience naturally flows from the heart of the disciple, as they learn and grow in their faith and understanding of all God has done for them.

Late into 1917, Oswald Chambers went home to be with Jesus at the unexpectedly young age of 43. Born in Aberdeen, Scotland, Chambers came to know the grace of God under the preaching of Charles Haden Spurgeon. Throughout his school and early ministry, Chambers was known for his vibrant and adamant will to live in obedience to God. At the outbreak of WWI, Chambers volunteered as a chaplain and went to Zeitoun, Egypt, to minister to the soldiers there. He said, "God's will can be found in any circumstance of life, so long as individuals are willing to have a personal relationship with Christ and completely abandon themselves to Him. The great word of Jesus to his disciples is *abandon*."[xxxiii]

Oswald Chambers' sermons and daily journals were later turned into a collection of daily devotions by his wife called *My Utmost for His Highest*. Oswald understood, to be a disciple of Jesus is to totally and completely abandon oneself.

God's saving grace elects, frees, informs, empowers, and sustains. By His grace, we can be disciples of Jesus Christ. Right belief produces right motivation, which enables righteous action.

Thoreau's statement makes discipleship slavery. I believe Chambers would have agreed with him. Discipleship is slavery. But slavery to Christ is the only true foundation of genuine liberty.

Sacrifice and Obedience are essential to the disciple. Without evidence of these marks, the salvation of any person is in question. However, these are nothing if unaccompanied by love.

Chapter 7: Love

The Theological Significance of Love

"The true soldier fights not because he hates what is in front of him, but because he loves what is behind him." – G. K. Chesterton

Love is mysterious. Its full definition escapes human understanding. We can recognize it, see it in others, feel it ourselves, but to completely define it is doubtful. For love ever surprises us. Just when you think you have it figured out, it shows a new facet of itself previously forgotten, underappreciated, or perhaps never seen before.

I married Janelle on May 27th, 2012. I remember walking into that Thomas Kinkade church auditorium to the Imperial March theme song from *Star Wars: A New Hope* with all my brothers, brothers-in-law, and best friend from high school. I was so in love I didn't even care if my nerd roots showed. My face was already sore from so much smiling. Then the music stopped. Complete silence. Everyone knew what to do. They stood.

Behind two white trimmed glass doors stood Janelle. She glowed. The doors opened, the music began, and escorted by her father, Janelle started to walk toward me. With every step, my heart increased in beats per minute. This was my lady, my wife, my love.

Janelle and I have been married seven years now. At the time of writing this chapter, we have been apart for over seventy-five days. I can tell you honestly, I love her more at this moment then when I looked upon her behind those glass doors. We have three blessings from God. Maggie, Audrey, and Emma. The love that these three beautiful little girls' control in me is dangerous. They don't yet realize it, but they have all 6' 3" 205 pounds of Daddy in the palm of their tiny little hands.

Where does this come from? Why do we feel this way? Why is it that some lose this feeling? What is the theological significance of love?

The definition of love is as mysterious as God. For God is love (1 John 4:16). To be a disciple is to love. To know Jesus is to know love. To believe in God is to believe in love. To obey God is to love. To live for God is to love. There is no salvation where there is no love.

In this chapter, we will explore the theological significance of love.

We will examine God's love within the Trinity, creation, law, His Son, and revelation. What we will see is God's definition of love compared to western cultures. Ultimately, we will see that humanity finds its meaning in God's revelation of love.

Love in the Trinity

God pictures love perfectly in Himself. God is one and exists in three persons: Father, Son, and Holy Spirit. The Father is fully God, the Son is fully God, and the Spirit is fully God. God is one. I don't pretend to fully understand it, but I completely believe it. Within the Trinity is the perfect display and exchange of love. First, let us look at the Trinity itself.

My goal is not to complete a robust theology of the Trinity, but rather a basic understanding to illustrate the perfect love that each person demonstrates for the other in the Godhead. Consider the following first on the singularity of God:

Deuteronomy 6:4-5 "Hear, O Israel: The LORD our God, the LORD is one. You shall love the LORD your God with all your heart and with all your soul and with all your might."

Isaiah 44:6 "Thus says the LORD, the King of Israel and his Redeemer, the LORD of hosts: "I am the first and I am the last; besides me there is no god."

1 Timothy 2:5-6 "For there is one God, and there is one mediator between God and men, the man Christ Jesus, who gave Himself as a ransom for all, which is the testimony given at the proper time."

Ephesians 4:6 "one God and Father of all, who is over all and through all and in all."

Scripture teaches that God is one. However, it also teaches that there are three persons, Father, Spirit, and Son in the one Godhead. These sections are too long to quote, but a reading of Romans 8, Ephesians 1:3-14, 2 Thessalonians 2:13-14, and 1 Peter 1:2 are sufficient for showing that all three persons are integral to salvation. However, the following sections are necessary to mention in length:

Matthew 28:19-20 "Go therefore and make disciples of all nations, baptizing them in the name of the Father and of the Son and of the Holy Spirit, teaching them to observe all that I have commanded you. And behold, I am with you always, to the end of the age."

John 8:58 "Truly, truly, I say to you, before Abraham was, I am."

John 20:28-29 "Thomas answered him, "My Lord and my God!" Jesus said to him, "Have you believed because you have seen me? Blessed are those who have not seen and yet have believed."

Romans 9:5 "To them belong the patriarchs, and from their race, according to the flesh, is the Christ, who is God over all, blessed forever. Amen."

Colossians 1:15-17 "He is the image of the invisible God, the firstborn of all creation. For by him all things were created, in heaven and on earth, visible and invisible, whether thrones or dominions or rulers or authorities—all things were created through him and for him. And he is before all things, and in him all things hold together."

Acts 5:3-5 "But Peter said, "Ananias, why has Satan filled your heart to lie to the Holy Spirit and to keep back for yourself part of the proceeds of the land? 4 While it remained unsold, did it not remain your own? And after it was sold, was it not at your disposal? Why is it that you have contrived this deed in your heart? You have not lied to man but to God."

Chapters could be written about these passages, and books have been published on their teachings. But if I can assume you agree with Christian orthodoxy, then you believe God is Trinity. Within the Trinity, there is perfect harmony and love. Everything God does he executes within perfect union of himself.

The first words of the Bible are mind boggling. Genesis 1:1 "In the beginning, God created the heavens and the earth." The beginning is referring to the creation of the earth. But before the beginning of the earth what was there? John answers that question.

John 1:1-4 "In the beginning was the Word, and the Word was with God, and the Word was God. He was in the beginning with God. All things were made through him, and without him was not any thing made that was made. In him was life, and the life was the light of men."

"Him" is Jesus in John's introduction. Before the heavens and earth, there was God. There was the Word. But there was also the Spirit. Genesis 1:2 "And the Spirit of God was hovering over the face of the waters." All three were present at creation, and all three existed before creation as the singular Godhead.

The pre-existence of God is incomprehensible. How long did God exist before creation? Who created God? The answers, "always and no one." He always has been and always will be. He exists perfect in and of Himself. He needs no relationships for He has a perfect relationship within Himself. This is a profound mystery, but if we consider the interactions within the Trinity that we have recorded, then we can piece together the exchange of love within the Godhead.

The Father loves the Son.

John 3:34-35 "For he whom God has sent utters the words of God, for he gives the Spirit without measure. The Father loves the Son and has given all things into his hand." God the Father has authority over everything. Yet, h does not withhold that authority from the Son. He gives it to Him generously and freely. John 5:20 "For the Father loves the Son and shows him all that he himself is doing. And greater works than these will he show him, so that you may marvel."

The Father does not keep any secrets from the Son. He shares with Him everything and includes the Son in His plans. More than that, the Father desires the Son to be honored as he is honored. John 5:22-23 "For the Father judges no one, but has given all judgment to the Son, that all may honor the Son, just as they honor the Father." The Father loves the Son through extending Him His authority over all things, including Him in His plans, and handing all judgment over to Him. The Father loves the Son and desires to glorify Him.

The Son loves the Father.

John 17:26, "I made known to them your name, and I will continue to make it known, that the love with which you have loved me may be in them, and I in them." The Son desires all to the glorify the Father. His goal is that mankind might know the name of God. In other words, that we might know who the Father is as the Son knows Him. His majesty, His holiness, His wrath, His love, His kindness, His strictness, His compassion, His anger, His patience, His joy. John 14:13, "Whatever you ask in my name, this I will do, that the Father may be glorified in the Son." John 17:1, "Father, the hour has come; glorify your Son that the Son may glorify you." The Son goes to His death willingly so that the Father may be glorified. The death of Christ is as much, if not more, about the glory of the Father as it is about the salvation of man. The Son loves the Father and desires to glorify Him.

The Father and the Son are united in their love for the Spirit and the Spirit for the Father and the Son.

1 John 4:7-13 "Beloved, let us love one another, for love is from God, and whoever loves has been born of God and knows God. Anyone who does not love does not know God, because God is love. In this, the love of God was made manifest among us, that God sent His only Son into the world so that we might live through him. In this is love, not that we have loved God but that he loved us and sent His Son to be the propitiation for our sins. Beloved, if God so loved us, we also ought to love one another. No one has ever seen God; if we love one another, God abides in us and His love is perfected in us. By this, we know that we abide in him and he in us, because he has given us of His Spirit."

John uses God's interpersonal love to address why we are supposed to love others. We will address this in greater detail later. But examining this passage we see John's rich theology of the

Trinity's love. Verses 12 and 13 are crucial to understanding the Spirit's love.

On this passage, John Piper says, "God is love because from all eternity love has been the Spirit uniting the Father and the Son... The evidence of being indwelt by the Spirit of God is the experience of loving Jesus the way the Father loves him."xxxiv In other words, the Spirit is constantly uniting the Father and the Son in love for each other. The Spirit's love for the Father and the Son is magnified as the Spirit produces worship in those whom the Spirit indwells. And the Father and Son love the Spirit, and send the Spirit to believers that they might know that God is love.

Alright, at this point you are likely somewhat confused. Let me reassure you, that is okay. You probably have more questions now than before you first started reading. I have more now than before I started writing. However, what is clear through this complexity, is that there is a complete, perfect, mutual, and continual exchange of love within the Godhead.

These verses attest to a desire within the Godhead to magnify and glorify the other. The theological significance is apparent. We cannot understand God apart from His interpersonal love. He is defined by perfect love.

Let me add one caveat. God is love. But love is not God. Today people are solving all problems and controversies with "just love one another." Love is an ever-present quality within the Godhead. Love fuels God's plans and purposes. Though it might be hard to accept, God's wrath is a form of His love. Love for His glory, and love for our holiness. Our understanding and definition of love must come from God's objective Word, rather than cultures ever changing opinions.

The question then should be asked, if God is perfectly satisfied in His interpersonal love relationship within the Godhead, why creation?

Love in Creation

My favorite childhood house growing up was on Whidbey Island. We lived on several acres that backed up to a deep evergreen and alder forest. I have many memories of bonfires, tree forts, zip lines, motorcycles, and pretending to be a Jedi in and around that house. One memory I will never forget was when I was ten. My bedroom was on the second story and I positioned my twin bed directly under the roof skylight so that I could look at the stars as I was falling asleep. This memory wasn't of me imagining I was Luke Skywalker fighting with the rebellion. I had many of those. I remember looking up at those stars at the age of ten and wondering, why are we here? If God made us, why did He?

I am not the only one to look up to the heavens and ask these sorts of questions. Psalm 8:3-4 says "When I look at your heavens, the work of your fingers, the moon and the stars, which you have set in place, what is man that you are mindful of him, and the son of man that you care for him?" David asked the same thing and probably so have you.

We have already explored at length how God is completely satisfied relationally in and of Himself. He needs nothing. And no one can add anything to who he is. Why then creation? What is the purpose of the stars, the earth, the trees, the waters, the animals, and living things? Why did God create us if He needed nothing from us?

Our minds have difficulty understanding this, since the vast majority of things we create are done so to fill some internal need. Whether that be physical, for life or shelter, or emotional for entertainment and enjoyment. Human creations are vastly centered on self-need. However, God's creation isn't about what he needs, but rather is a reflection of who he is.

God did not create life because he was lonely, bored, self-absorbed, or needed anything, but rather because he is love. Due to His perfect character, God foreordains all things in His perfect plan, to fulfill His perfect purpose. His character, plan, and purpose are all centered on love.

Think about all the things God has created. Taste buds for example. Why did God create taste buds on our tongues? And with such detail! We can taste the smallest differences in five large categories, all for what? Well, one reason is undoubtedly so we could know what tastes like food and what does not, so we don't mindlessly crunch on dirt. But primarily for enjoyment. The Bible speaks of the promise land as a place flowing with milk and honey. Two things that are wonderful to taste and represent pure prosperity.

Consider sex. The level of detail and intricacy that God created the activity of sex with is astonishing. It very well could have been a bland, uninvolved, non-erotic activity that only occurred at certain times to initiate the reproductive cycle. But instead, God has created sex to be a form of intense enjoyment, to unify a husband and wife in surrender for each other. God chose to create sex to be an emotionally exciting experience for His creatures. All because he loved them.

We can continue to list all the things God has created and find the imprints of love on them all. God is love, and what he has created is meant to know and reflect who he is.

Why am I here? Why was I created? I am here because of God's love! I was created to know the love of God in His son Jesus

Christ, which results in glorifying and enjoying Him forever.

The Westminster Catechism summarizes humanity's purpose neatly. What is man's chief end? Man's chief end is to glorify God and to enjoy Him forever.

But I have skipped something, haven't I? What about the law? Is the law love? How can something that commands such cruel punishments, for what seems like meaningless mishaps, be loving? How can the object that has caused so much pain and death, reflect God's unmatched love? After the Fall, didn't God turn from love to legality?

Love in the Law

Old Testament law is the most scrutinized subject amongst present day atheists. It is considered to be the harshest, most barbaric, foolish document that has imprisoned millions of people in primitive thinking and living for centuries. It is ridiculed as only bringing about hate. Any god who commands such a law cannot be love.

Richard Dawkins in his book *The God Delusion* said, "The God of the Old Testament is arguably the most unpleasant character in all fiction: jealous and proud of it; a petty, unjust, unforgiving control-freak; a vindictive, bloodthirsty ethnic cleanser; a misogynistic, homophobic, racist, infanticidal, genocidal, filicidal, pestilential, megalomaniacal, sadomasochistic, capriciously malevolent bully."[xxxv]

Before he passed, Christopher Hitchens said in his book *god is Not Great: How Religion Poisons Everything,* that he will leave it to the faithful to "burn each other's churches and mosques and synagogues, which they can be always relied upon to do." Hitchens saw the commands of the Old Testament as an abusive regulatory system created by punitive, oppressive, genocidal man to control and validate their cruelty.^{xxxvi}

These two prevalent atheists are representatives of the large and ever-growing following who share their sentiment. For most, they cannot see one ink stain of love in the law of God. Every true disciple of Christ should wrestle with these statements made by these men and those who share their view. Does their perspective anger you? Are you indifferent to their words? Or have you fallen into the postmodern mindset that this is their free perspective and it has no effect on you, and therefore demands no response? Anger, indifference, or open compliance can all be devastating responses to such attacks on the character of God. Disciples of Christ are called upon to rightly represent the truth of God in action and word.

Paul instructs Timothy, "preach the word; be ready in season and out of season; reprove, rebuke, and exhort, with complete patience and teaching. For the time is coming when people will not endure sound teaching, but having itching ears they will accumulate for themselves teachers to suit their passions and will turn away from listening to the truth and wander off into myths. As for you, always be sober-minded, endure suffering, do the work of an evangelist, fulfill your ministry" (2 Tim. 4:2-5). Every disciple of Christ should be ready to accurately reason the love of God present in His law.

The law is love. Before examining God's law of love, step back with me and consider the purpose of the law.

The law as a guardian. In the letter to the Galatians, one of Paul's topics is to address misconceptions and false teachings concerning God's law. In Chapter 3:15-29 he focuses his discussion on the purpose and use of the law. In verse 19, Paul says, "Why then the law? It was added because of transgressions." In Romans 3:19 Paul clarifies this more, "Now we know that whatever the law says it speaks to those who are under the law, so that every mouth may be stopped, and the whole world may be held accountable to God." The law showed our transgressions, functioning as a "guardian until Christ came, in order that we might be justified by faith" (Gal. 3:24). The law provided the lenses needed to see our sin, for "sin is not counted where there is no law" (Rom. 5:13).

As a guardian, the law not only addressed what we should and should not do, but what to do when the law is broken. God institutes the sacrificial system. This system is rightly described by atheists as horrific, bloody, grotesque, animal cruelty, and repulsive. It was designed to be all these things. The sacrificial system was meant to assault every human sense.

From a young age, every person was taught by visually seeing, hearing, feeling, tasting and smelling the penalty for sin, which is death. "For the wages of sin is death" (Rom. 6:23). God's love for His people produced a means to atone for sin, sacrifice. But the sacrificial system was only meant to point to the need for a future final sacrifice. As Romans 3:20 says, "For by works of the law no human being will be justified in his sight, since through the law comes knowledge of sin."

The law was never designed to save anyone. It was given as a loving road map that leads to the one who can give life! Under the law, humanity sees their undeniable separation from God and their need of Jesus Christ. Galatians 3:24-25 says, "So then, the law was our guardian until Christ came, so that we might be justified by faith. But now that faith has come, we are no longer under a guardian." The law was God's loving kindness to guide His people to faith in Christ.

Was the law arbitrary then? Did God decide to make up a lot of rules that could later be broken just to make humanity more sinful? Isn't it cruel rather than loving to so restrict a person's freedom and imprison them in a system of rules and regulations?

Let's ask this instead. Why do parents tell their children not to play in the street? Doesn't this encroach on their freedom? Why do parents make kids eat vegetables before giving them dessert? Isn't that demonstrating cruel regulations on their diet? Why do parents make their children do their schoolwork? Isn't this forcing unwanted indoctrination upon a free-thinking soul? Why is it that parents feel justified in saying "because I said so" to support their commands? Isn't this a form of repressive megalomaniacal egotistical arrogance to presuppose that kind of authority? Why do parents tell their children to put a coat on before going outside in the winter? Isn't this restriction upon items of clothing demonstrating dictatorship? Why do parents mandate their children to attend practices, rehearsals, and play on sports teams? Isn't this a forced physical, emotional, financial, and time-consuming sacrificial system? For the majority of parents, they do these things because they love their children and desire the best for them.

The law is meant for our best.

The law is the manifestation of the absolute love of a Father who desires the best for His children. Unlike human parents however, this Father knows exactly what is perfect for His children. His love is fully informed by His righteousness and justice, and therefore is the purest richest love that can be known. The Father's love can be specifically seen in the Ten Commandments.

Every one of the Ten Commandments centers on a relationship. The first four commands are between God and man while the last six focus on humanities relationship with each other.

The most loving thing God gave us is Himself. The first four commandments focus God's prescription for an undefiled relationship with Him.

First, we are to have no other gods. Nothing else can satisfy our created desire than to be in relationship with the true sovereign God.

Second, we are not to make any idols. Idolatry drives our hearts away from knowing the fullness of God.

Third, we are not to take the name of God in vain. It is to be kept holy.

Fourth, we are to keep the Sabbath holy. The day of rest signifies our trust in God to sustain us, and to remember His works.

These four commandments all revolve around keeping God the premier focus of our lives. As our creator, God alone knows when we are completely committed to Him. Only then will we discover genuine joy and happiness. But our relationship with God is directly affected by our interaction with others.

God commands loving relationships with others.

First, honor your mother and father. Paul says this is the first command with a promise in Eph. 6:2. To keep honor for father and mother requires humility and to give precedence to one's parents over oneself, especially as child becomes an adult and must see to the care of their parents.

Second, you shall not murder. In Matthew 5:21-26 Jesus clarifies for us that anger itself is murder. Therefore, our hearts should seek peace with our fellow man.

Third, we shall not commit adultery. As Jesus discusses, not to even look at a man or woman with lust in our hearts. Not only is our love for our spouse to be solely theirs, but we are also to respect and guard the love between others by purifying our thoughts.

Fourth, we are not to steal. Theft destroys relationships and escalates contention.

Fifth, we are not to bear false witness. Lying about others destroys people's reputations and potentially can backfire on the liar, leading others to no longer trust them.

Sixth, we are not to covet others possessions and life. This law centers around the gratefulness, contentment, and personal resolve to be satisfied in God alone.

The Ten Commandments all increase and properly guard love. Love for God and love for others. However, no one will see these laws as loving unless they are working with the same definition of love. As we have seen, the Christians definition of love is rooted in the character of God. Therefore, love in the law is hard to see when absent from the nature of God. But when we examine the law through the character and authority of the supreme God of the universe, love is embedded in every line.

Even laws that seem unreasonably restrictive, are acting as a guardian for God's people toward personal and communal fulfillment. The law of God is perfect and set to steer Israel toward holiness, so that they might know God and enjoy Him forever.

People outside of Jesus will never understand this. Unnecessary restrictions, such as sex only within marriage, will continually be called foolish by the world. Laws regarding church leadership and discipline will appear cultish and primitive. In reality, these voluntarily followed commands not only bring indescribable joy, but also prove our genuine discipleship.

Love in Jesus

A simple glimpse into the most well-known verse of scripture is all the articulation required to prove God's love for us in sending

His Son. John 3:16, "For God so loved the world, that he gave His only Son, that whoever believes in Him should not perish but have eternal life." The most misunderstood word in this verse is "world."

When John uses the term cosmos for world, he does not have a positive image in mind, nor even a neutral one. This term in John's usage is almost exclusively used to denote sinfulness and rebellion against God. In John 1:29, the author refers to Jesus as the one who will take away the sins of the world. John 3:17 and 4:42 show the world requires saving. In John 7:7, the world hates Jesus because He testifies against it. John 8:23, the world is opposite to Jesus, the two are fundamentally separated by sin. John 15:19, the world hates the disciples of Christ. 1 John 2:15-17 summarizes John's view succinctly.

"Do not love the world or the things in the world. If anyone loves the world, the love of the Father is not in him. [16] For all that is in the world—the desires of the flesh and the desires of the eyes and pride of life—is not from the Father but is from the world. [17] And the world is passing away along with its desires, but whoever does the will of God abides forever."

God's love for the world is incredible. His love isn't a momentary fleeting feeling. His love is an eternal decision he made, before ever creating a single stone. Ephesians 1:4 says, "he chose us in him before the foundation of the world." Amazing. He created everything, knowing Adam and Eve would rebel. Knowing that His people, Israel, would reject Him. Knowing that I would sin against Him. And in spite of all that, He loved us by giving us His son Jesus.

John 3:16 means that before all creation, God knew the world would be evil. Still He loved us, created us, and amongst the Trinity chose to send Jesus to die on the world's behalf. In Jesus, God's unconditional and purposeful love is displayed to unknowable depths. Romans 5:8 says it best, "but God shows his love for us in that while we were still sinners, Christ died for us." While we rejected Him, He died for us.

The disciple of Christ is called to model God's unconditional love in Jesus. The disciple of Christ must look at the world, with all its flaws and filthiness, and seek to have the eyes of God and love it. Jesus came for the dirtiest and most self-righteous. Within our regenerated hearts, we strive to mirror His love.

Love in Revelation

Lastly, God has loved us through revelation. Not only is the book of Revelation an outpouring of love, but all of the scriptures are God's loving revelation to the world.

God is not silent; He speaks through His written word. Hebrews 4:12 says, "For the word of God is living and active, sharper than any two-edged sword, piercing to the division of soul and of spirit, of joints and of marrow, and discerning the thoughts and intentions of the heart." God convicts hearts of sin and turns them toward forgiveness in Christ through the word. John attests that in the reason for His gospel, "these are written so that you may believe that Jesus is the Christ, the Son of God, and that by believing you may have life in his name" (John 20:31). God's word is a form of His love.

In God's word, we have everything we need to live a life of godliness. 2 Timothy 3:16-17 says, "All Scripture is breathed out by God and profitable for teaching, for reproof, for correction, and for training in righteousness, that the man of God may be complete, equipped for every good work." God doesn't leave us directionless. He lovingly provides for us everything we need to live for Him and find joy living in His truth.

God also has not kept us in the dark about the future. In the book of Revelation, God has outlined for us what will unfold. There will be a day of judgment. Jesus is coming back. And we will reign and rule with Him. We will be given new bodies, and there will be no more pain and death. This final hope provides immense comfort in times of pain and suffering.

Summary

The theological significance of love is rooted in God Himself. God's love is an unconditional, all-knowing, and everlasting love. He is faithful to His word and His promises. God's love is displayed in the Trinity, Creation, Law, Jesus, and Revelation.

This has been a heavier chapter. I understand it may have created more questions than answers. However, it is crucial to denote the supremacy of God's love. Jesus calls His disciples to love as He has loved. Culture will tell us to love those who deserve to be loved. Jesus tells you to love the least deserving.

In the next chapter, we will explore the specific measurements of Christian love in light of God's unconditional love in Christ.

Chapter 8: Love

A True Disciple will Love

"A new commandment I give to you, that you love one another: just as I have loved you, you also are to love one another. By this all people will know that you are my disciples, if you have love for one another." – John 13:34-35

Someone asked me awhile back, "Why do you do it?"

Slightly perplexed I responded with, "Do what?"

They continued, "Why do put yourself through unnecessary risk, pain, and suffering to go climb mountains?"

A boyish grin came across my face. I climb mainly because I love it. I was going to make a joke about loving misery. But thinking on it a second, my true reason came to me.

I responded, "It changes my perspective."

The ascent of a climb can be an incredibly inward focusing experience. Every inclined step is an opportunity to turn back, change direction, or feel sorry for yourself. When it is dark, cold, windy, snow blowing in your face, sometimes you just want it to end. Often the only thing you can do is just stare at your feet and take one more step. But once you reach the summit, all of the sudden, your vision widens. It's daytime, you can see other climbers struggling to get where you are. Looking up you can see other mountains, cities, and maybe even the ocean. That feeling on top is why I love climbing. And when I let my mind focus on the feeling of being at the apex, it fuels my feet for the ascent.

Not perfectly, but partially, I liken this to how Christians are fueled to love others. One of the most difficult things in life is to love. Life often gets in the way of love. Loving people can be hard when your late to work, the inbox is full, and you are behind on your latest assignment. Even loving your kids can be full on mortal combat, especially when the younger one won't stop crying because the older one is acting like Satan's minion. As I am writing this, I can hear two distinct cries coming from the kitchen as little wants and desires are not being met with immediate action.

The insane thing about Christianity, is Jesus hasn't called us to just love those who are loveable. Jesus calls His disciples to love as He has loved. He calls us to love both the loveable and the unlovable. He calls us to unconditional love of our dearest and closest friend as well as our most heinous and detestable enemy.

The task to love can be like the 2am point on a mountain ascent. It is dark, cold, windy, and turning in a different direction sounds like the most appealing option. The only way we can continue the climb, is when we set our minds on the apex of God's love for us. Grasping God's love for us will fuel our hands, feet, and lips to love others through the ascents and descents of life.

As the last chapter explained, the theological significance of love is intrinsically tied to the nature of God. Love is displayed in the Godhead itself, and every activity God participates in.

Particularly, God's love is revealed through the sending of the Son, Jesus Christ. Therefore, a true disciple of the Son of God is validated, in part, by their Christ-like love. 1 John 4:7-8 leaves no room for misunderstanding, "Beloved, let us love one another, for love is from God, and whoever loves has been born of God and knows God. Anyone who does not love does not know God, because God is love." Love is critical evidence of genuine discipleship. If a person has no Christ-like love in their life, then they have not partaken of it themselves, and their faith is found void.

This chapter will examine how God's multifaceted love is displayed in Christ, and how His true disciples will reflect this love in their lives. This reflection will not be an exact image. As creatures still wrestling with the consequences of sin, we will never fully image the love of Christ. The reflection of a genuine disciple is like a mirror. A mirror displays the one it reflects. It is not itself the object of its reflection, but it presents the image and glory of its object. Christians will not be able to produce the exact purity and holiness of Christ's love, but we will, if our faith is sincere, reflect it.

A True Disciple Seeks to Love Unconditionally

As Jesus loves unconditionally, His disciple will also seek to love.

Unconditional love is at the heart of the gospel message. However, the word itself is not found in scripture. Like the word *Trinity*, it is a word that has been grafted into Christian theology to denote a particular facet of God's love. Some theologians try to point to the Greek word ἀγάπη (Agape) as evidence of God's unconditional love. But there is nothing within the semantic range that is definitively unconditional. When compared with ἔρως (Eros) and φιλέω (Phileo), ἀγάπη "is a love which makes distinctions, choosing and keeping to its object... [a] free and decisive act determined by its subject."[xxxvii] Though the word is not distinctly unconditional, it is however selective.

It is within this selective understanding that theologians draw out the unconditional nature of God's love in Christ. Among the most apparent passages in scripture, is Paul's letter to the Romans.

In Romans, Paul progresses in his letter to portray the hopelessness of humanity's position and God's selective unconditional love. Romans 3:10 quotes Psalm 14:3, "None is righteous, no not one." He continues in verse 23, "for all have sinned and fall short of the glory of God." The reasoning is no one deserves life, no one deserves reconciliation, all people are depraved, and separated from God. However, verses 24-25, "are justified by his grace as a gift, through the redemption that is in Christ Jesus, whom God put forward as a propitiation by his blood, to be received by faith. This was to show God's righteousness because in his divine forbearance he had passed over former sins." What does this mean? Despite the condition of sinfulness, God sent Jesus to be the appeasement of His own wrath, so that we would not be consumed by it.

Later in Rom. 5:8 he explains it plainly, "but God shows his love for us in that while we were still sinners, Christ died for us." The love God displayed in sending Jesus was not conditioned upon our obedience or actions toward Him. He selectively chose to love us.

We discussed this before in previous chapters, but it is worth repeating. In his letter to the Ephesians, Paul explains the extent of God's unconditional love. In Eph. 2:4-6 Paul in the Spirit wrote, "But God, being rich in mercy, because of the great love with which he loved us, even when we were dead in our trespasses, made us alive together with Christ—by grace you have been saved." No offense is too great or small to penetrate the inseparable love of God through Jesus Christ. God has chosen to love us without condition. As Paul continues, he makes that clear, "for by grace you have been saved through faith. And this is not your own doing; it is the gift of God, not a result of works, so that no one may boast." God's love is an indescribable, undeserved, and unconditional gift.

Hold the phone, stop the theological train a second. Didn't you say I have to love to be a disciple? Isn't that a condition? Doesn't that disprove your previous point?

I have had several people ask me that before. The answer is no, it is not a condition of discipleship, it is a result of discipleship. Jesus never demands that people be loving before surrendering to Him. Instead, once a person surrenders to Christ, Jesus makes His home within them and begins to change that person from the inside out.

Therefore, when Jesus calls us to love as He has loved in John 13:34-35, He is calling us to something that only He can empower us to do. To love as Jesus has loved, requires the power of Christ to free us from the bondage of sin (Romans 5:18), and the Spirit to lead us into all righteousness (Gal. 5:16).

Jesus frees us and the spirit leads us to love unconditionally. As God looked at us and selectively chose to love us, we must do the same regardless of people's personalities, actions, or words toward us. The unconditional choice to love is incredibly difficult but wonderfully freeing. It is a decision you make without any thought of selfish reward.

Unconditional love is counter cultural. Unconditional love is unconcerned with what people can offer to me, but what I can offer to others. Many times, we base our relationships on things that we want and need, rather than what we can offer or supply.

Unconditional love is forward thinking. When we choose to love others because of God's love for us, it sparks intentionality in our relationships. Love is a conscious decision. A decision the regenerated heart desires to make! When you decide to pray for a person, that person will come to mind more often. When you are out shopping, they will come to mind. When you are going to an event or concert, they will come to mind. Suddenly, you will find that you are actively seeking ways to express love to this person simply because you chose to love them.

Unconditional love will completely change your marriage. If our love for our spouse is a choice rather than a reaction or flippant emotion to their actions or behavior, 95% of all marital problems will disappear.

Okay, yes, that was a made-up statistic. But I do believe the majority of marital problems are solved by both parties choosing to love the other.

Though seemingly unromantic in a western mind, this is the most powerful thing you can do for your marriage. When you choose to love based upon God's love for you, suddenly doing the dishes doesn't seem that bad. Cleaning the toilet seat becomes worship rather than worry. Changing a diaper turns from deplorable to a display of discipleship. Traditional relational love says, "if I do this for you, you better do this for me!" Unconditional love says, "Jesus did this for me, so I chose to do this for you." When your gaze is set upon the apex of Jesus' love, He will empower you to take another step in the ascent of unconditional love.

Unconditional love will change your relationship with your children. When you consciously decide to love your children regardless of what they want to do, what grades they receive, what music they like, and what friends they hang out with, something insane happens:

Your words and actions are no longer reactionary but visionary.

You will no longer become enraged when they do something that surprises you, because it is no longer about you. You have chosen to love them because of God's great unconditional love for you. When they mess up, your mind will go from "how could they do this to me?" to "how can I show them the love God has shown me?" When your child crashes your car, your mind will go from "how I am going to fix this?" to "how can I love them?"

When we love like Jesus every single relationship in our lives will experience drastic change. It won't be easy. It will hurt. It will be painful. It will bring suffering. Like a winter mountain climb, you will want to turn around and give up. But I want to encourage you, just keep stepping. Take one more step, and then another. Let the apex of God's love for you empower your every step on life's climb to love unconditionally. Occasionally, lift your head and look around at the beauty and majesty of a life defined by the love of Jesus. It can be a spectacular sight! And when you see those dark areas of lovelessness, walk toward them. Move in repentance toward those places and let the love of Jesus touch your temptation to be loveless.

A True Disciple will Seek to Love Humbly

As Jesus loves humbly, His disciple will seek to love.

The setting of John 13:34-35 is the upper room. Chapter 13 begins with a shocking account. In a perplexing unexpected manner, Jesus positions Himself as the household servant and begins to wash the disciple's feet. Peter took one look at what Jesus was doing and immediately said: "Lord, do you wash my feet?" After Jesus' response, Peter declares, "You shall never wash my feet." His stark statement is due to the unprecedented situation in front of Him. For no master washes his student's feet. Peter sees this as a breach of relationship, something that should never be done. He failed to understand Jesus was demonstrating what loving with humility looks like.

Loving with humility does not mean loving ignorantly with regards to position or power. Jesus is fully aware of who He is and what He deserves. He isn't teaching that everyone is the same so everyone should serve each other. He says plainly:

"Do you understand what I have done to you? You call me

136

Teacher and Lord, and you are right, for so I am. If I then, your Lord and Teacher, have washed your feet, you also ought to wash one another's feet. For I have given you an example, that you also should do just as I have done to you. Truly, truly, I say to you, a servant is not greater than his master, nor is a messenger greater than the one who sent him. If you know these things, blessed are you if you do them." – John 13:12-17

Jesus understands His position and power over the disciples. He is not one of them. He is above them. He is "Lord." This term in Greek culture refers to a person of superior position, power, or stature. But when combined with the Jewish context it has the possible implication of Jesus declaring Himself to be God. Yet, even though the disciples rightly should be serving Jesus, Jesus decides to demonstrate to them a humble form of service. He takes on the role of the lowest household servant and washes their feet.

A genuine disciple of Jesus will love with pure humility. This means loving someone with full knowledge of your social, political, familial, financial, or occupational superiority or inferiority. Position or power only provides a platform for further representation of Christlikeness.

A True Disciple will seek to Love Indiscriminately

As Jesus loved indiscriminately, so His disciple will seek to love.

John 13:21 "After saying these things, Jesus was troubled in His spirit, and testified, "Truly, truly, I say to you, one of you will betray me." Jesus demonstrates unprecedented humility by washing the disciple's feet. And yet, even more, He does so indiscriminately. Imagine the physical and emotional tension running through His fully human and divine veins as He washed Judas' feet. Jesus served the same man who was serving Him over to death.

Jesus teaches us to love our enemies. In Matthew 5:44-45 Jesus says, "Love your enemies and pray for those who persecute you, so that you may be sons of your Father who is in heaven." The Father looked upon the world, an enemy of holiness, and chose to love it by sending His Son. The genuine disciple displays their changed heart by loving as God has loved, they love their enemies. But His indiscriminate love does not stop with simply enemies.

All forms of discrimination are foreign to the redeemed heart. James 2 teaches us to reject the temptation of impartial treatment based upon wealth, class, or education. Jesus Himself in John 4 breaks cultural boundaries by engaging with a woman of Samaria. His action of having a simple conversation displays a stark rejection of any form of racism or cultural discrimination. No true disciple of Jesus can carry prejudice, racism, or bigotry while still carrying their cross. The cross itself is the greatest testament toward the complete inclusion of the gospel to all peoples.

In short, a true disciple will love indiscriminately, as they have been indiscriminately loved. Christians in today's culture cannot remain blind or unresponsive to the racial and social injustices happening all over the world. The cross demands uncontained inclusive love. The more a disciple discerns the indiscriminate love of the cross, the more fuel they have for each step of love in life.

Books have been written and organizations formed to address social injustice and mercy ministries. Christians absolutely should answer God's call to pray for, financially support, and participate in these ministries as God calls each of us. However, an important distinction needs to be made in terms of discipleship and indiscriminate love.

A disciple seeks to love indiscriminately so that God may be glorified and to introduce people to Jesus. Social and political agendas are not to be the disciples driving force. While providing health care, natural necessities, human worth, and other such mercy ministries are excellent and good, they cannot be divorced from the truth of the gospel. After Jesus fed the five thousand, He proclaimed hard and difficult truths to His audience. The result was most people walked away in disbelief and bewilderment at who he claimed to be (John 6:66).

Therefore, while a disciple must seek to love indiscriminately, them must equally love truthfully.

A True Disciple will seek to Love Truthfully

As Jesus loved truthfully, so His disciple will seek to love.

Jesus is equally indiscriminate as He is truthful. Culturally, we have lost our way when it comes to understanding these two aspects. Recently, I had a conversation with a co-worker about the gospel. We talked at length about the necessity of Jesus' death for our sin, and how without His sacrifice on our behalf we are in utter ruin.

At that point, he said, "Well that is true for you. But I do not believe it."

I asked him, "How can it be true for me, and not true for you?"

Essentially, he had bought into post-modernism and believed that in some sense, truth is determined by the individual.

To love indiscriminately does not mean to love untruthfully. The way Jesus loved was by declaring the exclusive truth inclusively.

Jesus said in John 14:6, "I am the way, and the truth, and the life. No one comes to the Father except through me." These words are polarizing. Jesus is stating plainly that He is the exclusive means of salvation. Contrary to popular teaching, there are not multiple paths that lead to God. World religions are not all blind men touching and describing the same elephant, from different vantage points. The only road up to the mountain, to heaven, is through the gate of repentance and surrender marked by the cross of Jesus Christ.

The truth is difficult to hear. It can feel offensive. However, to speak anything but the truth, is more unloving than to tell someone something more palatable. Imagine if my daughters wanted to touch the stove while the tea kettle was approaching a boil.

Normally I would tell them "No! You can't touch it because it will burn you."

But say I told them this, "Sweethearts, I am not going to tell you not to touch the stove. I don't want to be your judge, just your friend. We are both flawed people, after all, so you are free to touch what you desire."

The latter might sound loving and compassionate, but it is a coward's front that leads to extreme pain.

True disciples speak like Paul in Romans 1:16-17, "I am not ashamed of the gospel, for it is the power of God for salvation to everyone who believes, to the Jew first and also to the Greek. For in it the righteousness of God is revealed from faith for faith, as it is written, "The righteous shall live by faith." Never have Christians been called to passivity in terms of truth. We are to be the city set upon a hill so that all may look and be guided to the truth and praise God.

Thus, the true disciple seeks to love truthfully. The fear of man's opinions is greatly outmatched by the fear of their demise without ever hearing the truth of the gospel. Yes, we will be rejected by people when we love truthfully. We will lose family, friends, co-workers, jobs, and positions of power. But the cross of Christ compels us to love truthfully, for there is no other true way to love.

A True Disciple will seek to Love Forgivingly

As Jesus loved through forgiveness, so His disciple will seek to love.

Forgiveness is defeat and victory, surrender and conquest, to give up and to overcome. When a person forgives, they are laying aside their right to justice, punishment, retaliation, and vengeance. However, when a disciple forgives, they declare the victory, power, supremacy, and magnificence of God.

A true disciple will love by forgiving, as they have been loved by being forgiven. Colossians 3:13, "bearing with one another and, if one has a complaint against another, *forgiving* each other; as the Lord has *forgiven* you, so you also must *forgive.*" As we are to love because God has first loved us, so we forgive because e first forgave us. The motivation of forgiveness doesn't come from the remorse or repentance of the individual who committed the wrong. The reason for forgiveness is Jesus. Disciples do not forgive because someone has earned or deserves their forgiveness. We forgive because Jesus has forgiven us! Our love must carry on this unconditional nature even to complete forgiveness.

So, what exactly does it mean to forgive? Depending on who you ask, you will get many different answers. Dictionary.com understands the word to mean, "to grant a pardon, give up claim on account of, to grant pardon to, to cease to feel resentment too and to cancel a debt."xxxviii As you can tell within these five uses, several focus on a particular action where others refer to the emotion of the affected party.

In our culture, forgiveness is fuzzy. I have heard from friends, family, talk shows, movies, and political leaders versions of the following: "I have forgiven them, but I do not speak with them." While culture may accept that definition of forgiveness, is that what the biblical command to forgive has in mind? Is it a pure emotion with disregard to action; a legal action without regard to emotion; or a blend somewhere between the two? To truly understand the disciple's responsibility to forgive, we need to both understand the word and its reference point.

The Greek language has several words that we translate as forgive. The word χαρίζομαι (Charizomai) has roots tied to grace, meaning to give or grant something graciously. This is the word used in Col. 3:13. It is also used in Ephesians 4:32 when Paul tells the church at Ephesus, "Be kind to one another, tenderhearted, forgiving one another, as God in Christ forgave you." The reference here has clear action in mind. Something must be given or granted for forgiveness to have occurred. The standard is how we have been forgiven in Christ. As Christ now can look upon a sinner and call them saint, so a disciple must be able to look upon an offender as a friend.

Another word is ἀφίημι (Aphiemi) which means to pardon, to remove guilt from wrongdoing. God does not only forgive our wrong, but He also removes our guilt. Likewise, the disciple's forgiveness ought to make every effort to remove the sense of guilt from the offender. Unlike God, we cannot remove this for them, however, our demeanor, speech, and actions all must declare guiltless clemency.

Forgiveness is both action and emotion. We cannot say, "I forgave them in my heart, but I hope they die a painful death." Nor, "I forgive you, but will never talk with you again." Such statements are cultural definitions of forgiveness and not true Christ-centered forms of loving forgiveness. How then do we know when genuine forgiveness has occurred?

John Piper, in a sermon titled *As We Forgive Our Debtors*[xxxix], looks back to the Puritan Thomas Watson for his insight. Watson asked the following question and gave his response:

Question: When do we forgive others?

Answer: When we strive against all thoughts of revenge; when we will not do our enemies mischief, but wish well to them, grieve at their calamities, pray for them, seek reconciliation with them, and show ourselves ready on all occasions to relieve them.[xl]

Piper expounds on each part of Watson's definition for forgiveness.

1. **Resist thoughts of revenge:** Romans 12:19, "Never take your own revenge, beloved, but leave room for the wrath of God, for it is written, 'Vengeance is Mine, I will repay,' says the Lord."

2. **Don't seek to do them mischief:** 1 Thessalonians 5:15, "See that no one repays another with evil for evil."

3. **Wish well to them:** Luke 6:26, "Bless those who curse you."

4. **Grieve at their calamities:** Proverbs 24:17, "Do not rejoice when your enemy falls, and do not let your heart be glad when he stumbles."

5. **Pray for them:** Matthew 5:44, "But I say to you, love your enemies, and pray for those who persecute you."

6. **Seek reconciliation with them:** Romans 12:18, "If possible, so far as it depends on you, be at peace with all men."

7. **Be always willing to come to their relief:** Exodus 23:4, "If you meet your enemy's ox or his donkey wandering away, you shall surely return it to him."

143

Piper does superb service in bringing to mind Watson's clear explanation of biblical forgiveness. These seven points are excellent marking posts to measure if our forgiveness is genuine or faulty. Most people do not actively seek to pay evil for evil, perhaps more out of cowardice than out of holiness. However, few people will pray for their enemies, let alone seek to come to their relief. Yet, isn't this exactly what God has done for us in Christ? Jesus has petitioned on our behalf to the father. He gave Himself on behalf of the enemies of God. Our love must reflect the love of the one we follow!

Notice, nothing is said about anger or consequence. Piper follows his message by addressing the fact that sin should rightly cause anger in our hearts, and it will produce consequences. Paul instructs believers in Ephesians 4:26, "Be angry and do not sin." Piper says plainly, "Forgiveness is not the absence of serious consequences for sin."[xli] A disciple can actively forgive while pursuing criminal charges, just as a father can deeply love while punishing his child. Forgiveness is seeking the welfare of the other. For some people, the best thing is to receive the utmost physical judgment for their actions so that they may see their sin, turn, and receive the utmost forgiveness and pardon from God.

Summary

I had just sat down in the fifth row, center aisle, in Moody Bible Institute's chapel. Founder's week was typically held during the pinnacle of Chicago's February winter weather. Every year at this time, Moody brings in multiple pastors, professors, authors, and missionaries from around the world to charge students and the Christian community to continue to carry the passion for the Gospel which its founder, D. L. Moody, held dear. I still remember, after I put my winter coat under my chair, I pulled out the program and read the opening speakers name, Steve Saint.

I remember looking at the front where the speakers were sitting. There was an older gentleman, Caucasian, with greying hair, trimmed beard, and an oddly calm looking demeanor. Sitting next to him was an elderly native American looking man. He had large plug earrings and was wearing a mix of western and tribal clothing. One of my professors took the stage and began introducing our first speaker, a missionary to tribes in Ecuador.

As Steve began to share his story, he started by introducing us to his father and his four friends. Steve's father, Nate Saint and his friends Ed McCully, Pete Fleming, Jim Elliot, and Roger Youderian were missionaries, committed to bringing the gospel to the least reached in Ecuador. They had contacted the Huaorani tribe by Nate Saint landing their small aircraft on a sand bar on the Curary River, which they called "Palm Beach."

Two days after making initial contact, at roughly 3:00 p.m. on January 8, 1956, Nate, Jim, Ed, Pete, and Roger were speared to death by the Huaorani tribe, the very people they were trying to proclaim the gospel to.

Something seemed wrong as Steve spoke. He didn't seem angry, furious, or outraged about his father's death. He had an unnerving peace about him. But his story only began on January 8th. He then gestured to the first row of the auditorium, where the small older Native American man was sitting. He introduced him as Mincaye. Steve took a long pause. And then he looked around the auditorium and said, "this is the man who killed my father."

Through the divine providence of God and the faithfulness of the murdered men's surviving wives, Mincaye had become a reborn believer in Jesus Christ. Not only did he become a Christian, but he committed himself to help raise the children of the men he murdered. Steve went on to explain how he calls Mincaye "father", and his children call him "grandfather." When Steve was baptized, the man who presided over it was Mincaye. Mincaye went on to baptize both Steve's brother and sister.[xlii]

The love of Jesus Christ empowers radical forgiveness that defies reason. I remember sitting in that auditorium in absolute wonder at the goodness and love of God. The love of God can do what we think is impossible. Steve realized something at a young age. Life is not about our story. It is about God's story, and how the disciple can be used to help tell it.

True disciples of Christ will strive after his example. Imperfectly, but evidentially, a true disciple will love others unconditionally, indiscriminately, truthfully, humbly, and forgivingly. A disciple's extraordinary love comes from being extraordinarily loved. True disciples glance into the ever nearer future with Christ and interpret the reality around them, in light of the promise before them. Every step of misery, hardship, suffering, and intolerable people is given purpose by the promises of God. His love for us compels us to love others.

A true disciple will sacrifice, obey, and love as Christ has loved. The motivation for doing so comes from a full understanding of God's love toward us. Motivation is born from what we already possess in Christ.

The last mark of a genuine disciple is that they go and teach these things to others to make more disciples of Christ.

Chapter 9: Disciple

Theological Significance of Discipleship

"Always pass on what you have learned."

- Yoda

My earliest childhood photos are filled with lightsabers, Luke Skywalker outfits, and a barrage of Star Wars toys and trinkets.

I have an unusually vivid Star Wars memory from my childhood. It was a grey cloudy morning and I was shooting baskets outside my house on White Deer Lane. I missed a shot, and something incredible happened. The ball bounced off the rim and instead of running to go pick the ball up, I decided to try to use the force. I stretched out my hand, closed my eyes, and with every ounce of my 8-year-old body, I willed the ball to come to me.

And it did!

To my utter amazement, the ball slowly began to come. It then rolled faster and faster! It rolled straight past me into a ditch. It was then that I started to understand gravity, angles, and not everything is completely flat. Most of all, I understood then, I wasn't going to be a Jedi.

Regardless of its insane fantasy storyline, or its Buddhist roots, Star Wars has strong discipleship principles. To become a Jedi, you must have a Master. That Master is responsible to teach you how to be a Jedi. But it doesn't take place in a classroom. The Padawan (student), lives, eats, travels, and fights alongside their Master.

The lessons are not trivial, they are life. There is no place for theory and what if scenarios. The Master allows the student to apply what they have learned and is there to critique, encourage, and direct. Once the student is ready, then they will become a Master and go take on their own students.

Now before I jump down the George Lucas rabbit hole, I am not trying to say we should take theological implications from Star Wars. In no way am I saying that we should follow Yoda and Obi-Wan Kenobi in their style of discipleship. However, it does paint in cinematic form, an intriguing parallel to the process of discipleship.

The reason why people naturally understand this process, is God designed us to exist in these relationships. From the beginning, God has intended mankind to be discipled.

In this chapter, we will see how God has uniquely designed us for intimate discipleship relationships. By looking through the scriptures, we will discover the importance and process of biblical discipleship, specifically looking at the life of Christ.

To have an accurate evaluation of our discipleship, we must include the following truth: True disciples will disciple others.

Created to Disciple

In Genesis 1:28 God gives what has become known as the creation mandate, "Be *fruitful* and *multiply* and *fill* the earth and *subdue* it, and have dominion over the fish of the sea and over the birds of the heavens and over every living thing that moves on the earth." There has been significant discussion on this verse, but few conversations as it relates to God's intention for intimate discipleship relationships.

The command to "Be fruitful... multiply... and fill" all point to God's intention for humanity to expand through childbirth pre-fall.

God could have easily created millions or billions of people instantaneously. He could have created them all full grown with knowledge of life. But He didn't. He only made two. And He created them to bear children so that humanity would have dominion over all of creation.

For Adam and Eve to cooperate with this command, they bear the weight and responsibility of something wonderful and incredibly difficult. What they were tasked with, is one of the most neglected and delegated responsibilities today. Completing their task means their dedication to disciple their children.

God gifted Adam and Eve with children so that they could mirror Him. As they were taught, they could now teach. As God delighted in Adam and Eve's creation, so Adam and Eve are gifted with the delight of being creators of life and tasked to raise their children in what God has taught.

God's plan has always been for humanity to fulfill its purpose through intimate relationships that center themselves upon Him.

When the fall occurred, the necessity of discipleship exponentially increased. No longer would Adam and Eve only need to teach their children life skills and abilities to fulfill their command to subdue the earth. Now, they had the responsibility to explain why things are the way they are. Their children were born into sin and thus had to be taught how to understand it, interpret it, and what to do when they commit it.

God's purpose has always been for discipleship to begin in the home, continue in the church, and never cease until the world knows the name of Jesus.

Discipleship Begins in the Home

In Matthew 28:19 Jesus says, "Go therefore and make disciples of all nations..." This specific command of Jesus provides specific theological fruition to the principles of discipleship practiced for centuries amongst God's people. Although the Old Testament only uses the equivalent word once, the expectation and necessity of discipleship is present all over the pages of scripture. And God's process for discipleship has always started first in the home.

As a parent of three beautiful, amazing, energetic, but sinful girls, Janelle and I have both asked many times, "What does it look like to disciple our kids?" I am the first to raise my hand when someone asks, "Who here struggles with sin?" Parenting is a daunting and humbling task, let alone discipling amid our failures.

I will never forget years ago hearing Maggie's sweet tiny three-year-old voice tell me at the kitchen table, "Daddy, we don't say that word." I would love to tell you that was the only time my child corrected my speech or behavior, but that wouldn't match up with the whole obedience section of this book.

God calls us to disciple our children. But that call isn't with the appearance of perfection, rather it is with the humility, knowledge, and reliance upon grace and truth.

Grace and truth have always been the pillars upon which God's people have raised their children. Deuteronomy 6:4 is historically known as the Shema, the confession of faith. Though the confession was once only 6:4, it informally included verses 5-9; later in the second century A.D. these verses were formally added. It is as follows:

"Hear, O Israel: *The LORD our God, the LORD is one.* ⁵You shall *love* the LORD your God with all your heart and with all your soul and with all your might. ⁶And these words that I command you today shall be on your heart. ⁷You shall *teach them diligently to your children, and shall talk of them when you sit in your house, and when you walk by the way, and when you lie down, and when you rise.* ⁸ You shall bind them as a sign on your hand, and they shall be as frontlets between your eyes. ⁹ You shall write them on the doorposts of your house and on your gates."

You might not read this and immediately see grace. That is because many of us do not have a Jewish context and historical knowledge.

Look at the first part of the Shema, "The LORD *our* God, the LORD is one." While the emphasis of this verse is its theological significance of God's singularity, it also is a firm attestation to God's grace.

The sole creator and sustainer of the universe is *"our"* God. Israel's personal relationship with the true God cannot be lost upon our blog, tweet, post, or other media-saturated 21st century readers. For it recalls God revealing Himself to Abraham in Genesis 12-15, and graciously and unconditionally covenanting with Him. While Abraham was an unapologetic sinner and pagan, God chose to love him and reveal Himself to him. The Shema, while many things, is certainly a confession of faith in the grace of God.

The obvious section to our topic is verse seven of the Shema. But don't go there too quickly! If you go there without reading verses 5-6 you miss everything and will utter fail at verse 7. Too many professing Christian parents today ignore verse 5-6 and run to 7 whether they realize it or not! And I get it. For some, and perhaps you who are reading this, you came back to church because you had kids, and wanted to raise them right.

I have talked with many different young parents who find themselves back at church simply because they don't know what to do with their kids. They feel like the church is a pretty safe bet.

I remember sitting down with one young father who said, "I actually don't believe in all this church stuff. But I know that it teaches decent morals... I really just want my son to grow up with a good foundation... so I guess I am going to support what the church is teaching because I think it is the best for him early on." This sentiment, while sincere, causes nothing but guilt and confusion in a child and can even lead to complete rebellion.

True discipleship of our children requires daily commitment. Verse 5-6 says, "You shall love the LORD your God with all your heart and with all your soul and with all your might. And these words that I command you today shall be on your heart." In the Gospels, Jesus linked this to be the greatest commandment (Matt. 22:37; Mark 12:30; Luke 10:27).

To live this way is to bask in faith and grace. For we all fail daily at this command. We do not love God with all our heart, soul, and mind. Let that sink in for a second. Personally, every day, you will fail at loving God the way you are commanded to. When we let the reality of our sin permeate our vision, we begin to see the cross as we ought too.

The good news is Jesus loved God with all His heart, soul, mind, and strength. He has done this for us, and He has done this for your children. He is perfect and can bear the weight of this command. We participate in His perfection as we place our faith in Him.

Discipleship at home starts with humbly acknowledging our imperfections and our need for Jesus.

"Daddy, you got spankings when you were little, didn't you?" said Audrey, looking at me with her genuinely inquisitive big hazelnut eyes.

"Yes Audrey, Daddy got spankings for disobeying," I remember pausing here. I knew what I needed to say to Audrey to teach a valuable lesson, but I was afraid of what would follow.

"Audrey... did you know Daddy still disobeys too? Just like you and Maggie. Did you know that Audrey?" I had to tell her, she needed to know that I too disobey.

"But Daddy, who gives you spankings now?" The smile on my face was unavoidable. I was trapped by my 3-year-old with a deeply theological and pressing question. I knew it was coming and yet I walked right into her trap.

If we don't acknowledge our sinfulness, then we are denying the truth (1 John 1:8), and we are not demonstrating for our children reliance upon grace. Parenting in grace and truth requires us to be deeply honest with our sinfulness, and fervently place our trust in Jesus Christ.

Discipleship in the home focuses on Loving God as Jesus Loved.

Once we acknowledge our need of Jesus, we can embrace His grace to Love God as He did. We are to love God with all our heart, soul and strength. As discussed in the last chapter, this love is wild, baffling, insane, and total. It is a love that defies human logic and reason. This type of love for God inspires and motivates a love for His created people. And this love for His creation is to be shown equally to family and friends as it is to enemies and adversaries. A love that compels us to surrender what we most value and treasure to gain more of Him.

Discipling in our homes means speaking and displaying love for God. This can happen at the morning breakfast table, the weekly taxi shuttle rides, the weekend fun trip to the beach or hike in the mountains. The practical implications of these theological truths will be discussed in greater detail in the next chapter. However, it is imperative to allow this principle to root into your soul. Discipleship begins at home. And it begins by acknowledging our sinfulness and embracing Jesus' grace to love God as He did.

Now we are ready for verse 7.

Verse 7 encompasses discipleship in the home, "You shall teach them diligently to your children, and shall talk of them when you sit in your house, and when you walk by the way, and when you lie down, and when you rise."

The verb "Teach" is the Hebrew word שָׁנַן (*šā·nǎn*) which means to teach by repetition, say again or repeat. Some sources cite its meaning as having a "focus on 'sharpening' the student to be potent for action, as a sharp blade is able to cut."[xliii]

Discipleship at home is formal and informal instruction of God's word.

As parents, we are to speak God's word every day and in every way to our children. Our times of instruction should be both formally scheduled and informally practiced.

We should have formal times of instruction where we "teach them **diligently** to your children" (Deut. 6:7a). Formal scheduled times of discipleship will look different depending on the circumstances surrounding the home. Whatever the environment or current life chaos, it is critical not to surrender formal instruction of God's word to your children. Scheduling a specific time, even if only for 5 to 10 minutes, every day to sit and read and discuss scripture can be huge in a child's spiritual development. This is just a starting point.

Formal instruction should be conducted diligently. Develop or follow an instructional plan to walk them through the New Testament or the whole Bible in a year. Put aside several weeks to cover major doctrines of the faith. Plan out a study on Church History. Make this time age appropriate. If your home has significant age gaps, perhaps allow the older children to lead this time of study for the younger. Explore creative ways to engage your children and allow them to interact and ask questions. If they can't explain the Trinity after the third week that is okay. Remember, this is life. The long game of formal instruction to help them become a follower of Jesus and love God as His Son did.

Informal practiced discipleship happens as we go about our day; "[you] shall talk of them when you sit in your house, and when you walk by the way, and when you lie down, and when you rise" (Deut. 6:7b). This is taking advantage of situations and events to speak truth into your children's hearts. From times sitting watching a show or sporting event, to walking by the way in the grocery store, or as you are dropping them off at school. The true words of God should be flowing out of your speech. When their head hits the pillow, the last things they should hear are the true words of God. When they wake up in the morning, they should hear God honoring words.

Now I don't think the image here is of stale repetition of scripture's words. Your home does not have to sound like a continual Gregorian chant. Nor do you have to quote scripture incessantly to children. Also, be careful if the only time you talk about the Bible is when you are disciplining your children. These can cause resentment, rather than joy.

The point is the continual confirmation of scriptures meaning. While memorizing scripture is essential and should be practiced, that doesn't necessitate making them recite verses through the aisles of Walmart or withholding "screen time" until Psalm 1 is spoken perfectly from memory. Instead, consider informally communicating decisions and conversations with God's truth.

"Daddy, I stuck my tongue out today at school..." Maggie said and then trailed off looking out the window, not making eye contact with me. We had been talking all that week about not sticking our tongue out at anyone, no matter what they do to us.

At this moment riding back from school, I had a choice, be angry with her disobedience or rejoice in her honesty. But both of those decisions, right or wrong, rise from my emotions, rather than God's true word. If I want to know what I ought to say to my sweet little convicted five-year-old, then I need to allow God's truth to speak.

Instead of just saying, "That's okay, we mess up sometimes, do better tomorrow okay Maggie?" which reinforces moralism, I want to search for a response that elevates her understanding of God's word.

Something like this is more aligned to scripture, "Maggie, you know God has said to obey your parents. Sticking out your tongue is disobeying your Mom and I. At the same time, God is truth and we are told to be truthful people. Thank you for telling the truth, Maggie. God's word says, if we are truthful and say we sinned, God will forgive us. Since you were truthful with me, let's be truthful with God, and tell Him about that sin, and ask for His help to no longer stick your tongue out."

Immediately, you will notice the dialog between the first paragraph and the second is drastically different in both content and length. The first paragraph requires only 11 words, whereas the second takes 86. That is over an 800% increase in words to address the same situation. Bottom line, discipleship takes work. It is easier to just respond to situations according to emotional impulses. To interact according to God's truth requires you to walk by the spirit so you will not carry out the desires of the flesh (Gal. 5:16).

We were created to disciple. That discipleship begins at the home. To boil it down, discipling our children is the wonderful elegant dance of grace and truth. The dance is a continual acknowledgment of sin while seeking to embrace God's grace to love Him as Jesus did.

Christian discipleship begins in the home but must continue in the church. Every Christian has a spiritual fuel tank that is filled by more of Jesus. We help each other fill those tanks as we disciple one another to be like Christ.

Discipleship Continues in the Church

This one seems obvious. I mean of course, discipleship should exist in the church, right? Yes, it is obvious, and sadly it is often neglected. We will look at practical ways to facilitate a culture of discipleship in the next chapter.

First, let's take a moment and look at the start of the church. The church begins to grow as the truth of Jesus is preached. We read the following in Acts 2:42-47:

"And they devoted themselves to the apostles' teaching and the fellowship, to the breaking of bread and the prayers. [43] And awe came upon every soul, and many wonders and signs were being done through the apostles. [44] And all who believed were together and had all things in common. [45] And they were selling their possessions and belongings and distributing the proceeds to all, as any had need. [46] And day by day, attending the temple together and breaking bread in their homes, they received their food with glad and generous hearts, [47] praising God and having favor with all the people. And the Lord added to their number day by day those who were being saved."

The church's birth was founded upon the entangling lives of disciples of Jesus. The word we know of now as "church" simply means the assembly. The church was the assembly of believers in Jesus Christ who resolved personally and corporately to live for Jesus Christ.

Let me shift gears a second. Have you ever tried to get on a strict diet, start a workout plan, or learn a language? If you have, then you know the power of a united community. When you try to diet, and everyone around you is eating anything they want to stuff their pieholes with, it can make dieting incredibly difficult. Switch it up, if two or three others are around you on that same diet, watching you, refereeing you, and encouraging you not to eat that strawberry cheesecake, things tend to get a little easier and more enjoyable.

Here is an experiment. Walk into a CrossFit gym during one of the scheduled training sessions. It is truly an amazing study on humanity's natural craving for community. Inside, you will find people utterly hazing themselves. They are doing burpees, muscle ups, sprints, and pushing themselves to exhaustion. But watch them after it is over. They love it. They are smiling, laughing, high fiving, and congratulating each other. Why? Because they are united around the same goal of personal sacrifice for the sake of fitness.

Language is the same way. Try learning a language and never speaking to an actual person in that language. Hopeless. Pointless. Give up and learn the piano. But what happens when you immerse someone into a culture where everyone speaks that language? Suddenly, the urge to communicate, to be known, appreciated, valued, and understood, compels the mind to adapt and learn something completely foreign.

Humanity was created to be in relational community. God designed us to need each other. But not for dieting, fitness, or even to verbally communicate. He designed us to communally find our joy and purpose in Him together. Discipleship is the continual encouragement, prodding, compelling, and urging of the community to sacrifice, obey, love, and disciple others.

The Church is the hive of this activity of discipleship. Have you looked at a beehive for a while? I find them fascinating. Activity never ceases. They are constantly moving, shifting, buzzing, and working. It seems exciting. That is the church. It is a hive of individuals saved by the gospel of Jesus Christ, moving, shifting, buzzing, and working to encourage each other to live for Jesus and to tell as many people as possible about Him. This activity happens organically as the Spirit moves, compels and convicts us.

Listen to this description of the church from Acts 4:32-35:

"Now the full number of those who believed were of *one heart* and *soul,* and no one said that any of the things that belonged to him was his own, but they had everything in common. [33] And with great power, the apostles were giving their testimony to the resurrection of the Lord Jesus, and great grace was upon them all. [34] There was not a needy person among them, for as many as were owners of lands or houses sold them and brought the proceeds of what was sold [35] and laid it at the apostles' feet, and it was distributed to each as any had need."

A discipling church is a united church. They were of "*one heart* and *soul.*" This pictures the church as a living organism. The collective body of believers had one heartbeat.

Notice something. That heartbeat wasn't a building. The heartbeat wasn't a stage. The heartbeat wasn't lighting. The heartbeat wasn't children's programs. The heartbeat wasn't music. The heartbeat wasn't office space. The heartbeat wasn't even coffee! Amazing they did all this without caffeine!

The heartbeat was Jesus! They loved Jesus. They worshiped Jesus. They wanted more of Jesus. They prayed to Jesus. They sang to Jesus. They sold their property for Jesus. They were together to become like Jesus. They wanted other people to know Jesus. It is all about Jesus!

Discipleship in the church is as natural as honey to a beehive. If it is a hive, there will be honey. If it is a church, there will be discipleship. And the marks of genuine discipleship is being S.O.L.D. out for Christ.

Discipleship Never Stops

The hive doesn't stop buzzing even when the whole world is filled with honey! Alright, I took the analogy in a weird direction there, but you get my point. Discipleship never stops.

The great commission is clear. The disciple's task is to make more disciples. The Christians task is to make more Christians. Remember, those two sentences are the same.

Just before Jesus ascended, he said, "you will be my witnesses in Jerusalem and in all Judea and Samaria, and to the end of the earth." If you remember, Jesus said that something had to happen before the end comes.

Matthew 24:14 says, "and this gospel of the kingdom will be proclaimed throughout the whole world as a testimony to all nations, and then the end will come."

It is a mistake to take Acts 1:7 and Matthew 24:14, and conclude that discipleship ceases once the end comes. Not at all! We may as well get good at discipling, because we are going to do so for the rest of eternity.

When John was given his revelation from God, he saw a lot of strange things. It is like a Harry Potter movie on steroids. Horsemen of the Apocalypse, dragons trying to eat babies, and a bunch of scrolls, bowls, trumpets, swords and whatnot. There is significant deep truth in the pages of Revelation. I am not smart enough to know them all. But chapter four does help us when thinking about discipleship in heaven.

Revelation 4:8 says, "And the four living creatures, each of them with six wings, are full of eyes all around and within, and day and night they never cease to say, "Holy, holy, holy, is the Lord God Almighty, who was and is and is to come!"

For all of eternity these creatures are saying the same thing repeatedly. Holy, holy, holy, is the Lord God Almighty, who was and is and is to come. Forever, their entire purpose is to proclaim the holiness and supremacy of God! Whenever these creatures proclaim God's supremacy, something else happens.

Revelation 4:9-11, "and whenever the living creatures give glory and honor and thanks to him who is seated on the throne, who lives forever and ever, [10] the twenty-four elders fall down before him who is seated on the throne and worship him who lives forever and ever. They cast their crowns before the throne, saying, [11] "Worthy are you, our Lord and God, to receive glory and honor and power, for you created all things, and by your will they existed and were created."

Now if you're like me, your immediate question is, "how do they keep casting their crowns before the throne?" It must be a one-off, right? Or maybe they cast them, then go pick them up again to get ready for the next round? I chalk this up to one of those wait and see things.

The point is this. If the six creatures and the twenty-four elders are vigorously and continually engaging in discipleship activities (proclaiming the truth of God), then we should not expect anything different for ourselves.

As we live in heaven we will obey and love God forever. The new heavens will include work, buildings, and parties, through which we will continue encouraging each other in our praise and worship of God. Chief among our daily events will be the joy of collectively worshiping God.

Much of heaven is a mystery. But to be sure, most discipleship activities will not stop.

Summary

I am convicted in the writing of this chapter. Sadly, many professing Christian parents have left the responsibility of discipling children to the church. Perhaps, this is your story. You never had a parental example of discipleship in your home growing up. And now you have children, and you are not sure where to start.

As God's grace has saved us, it sustains us, and empowers us to disciple others. The beauty of grace is that your actions don't have to be perfect. Jesus was perfect for you. You have to be obedient. Trust in God and start discipling. He will take care the results.

As a father, I am to mirror my heavenly father, and impart to my children the truth of God. I am supposed to work at creatively teaching them the scriptures at age appropriate levels. Discipleship begins in the home. The better I disciple my children in the home, the more powerful and equipped they will be to disciple in the church.

One of the scariest days as a youth pastor was when the father of a 17-year-old senior asked to meet for lunch. I wasn't nervous about meeting with a parent, I was delighted. I loved to meet with parents and talk through how I can assist them in their discipleship of their children. What was scary about this lunch was the content the father wanted to discuss.

I was twenty-four at the time, and this respected father was in his late forties. I remember he looked at me with desperation.

"I have lost him. He won't listen to me anymore. I have pretty much given up at this point. My only hope is that you can get through to him."

He was right, he had lost his ability to influence his son.

I sat there scared. I wasn't scared by what he was saying. I was scared because I saw myself in his position. I knew this man loved his son, prayed for his son, and wanted to do anything to help his son follow Jesus. But he was powerless.

Unfortunately, life has a way for shifting our focus from what truly matters to secondary tasks and responsibilities. We can become so focused on our education, job, organization, hobbies, or social life that we forget the most important things. Teaching people who Jesus is and how to follow Him. This is one of the most important things we can do with our time. Especially, when that person is our son or daughter. But where do we start? How we go about this practically?

In the next chapter we will look at the process of disciple making as portrayed in scripture.

Chapter 10: Disciple

A True Disciple will Disciple

"By this my Father is glorified, that you bear much fruit and so prove to be my disciples."

– John 15:8

I am not a gardener. Plain and simple. Most things I try to plant end up dying. I am not trying to be modest. Last summer I purchased over $200 worth of fruit trees and plants. All dead. Granted, Axel, my 2-year-old German Shepherd-Husky mix, ate half of those plants. Still, the other half didn't have a chance.

Building a garden takes time, precision, effort, and knowledge. Usually, it doesn't happen over-night. And if it does happen over-night, there is a solid chance it won't last many nights.

When Jesus addresses the disciples in the upper room he uses the analogy of a garden. He calls Himself the true vine and the Father the vinedresser. We are the branches connected to the vine. Now I am not a gardener, but I see where He is going. The vine pulls up the nutrients provided from the soil, that the vinedresser maintains. The vine then fuels the branches to produce fruit. Jesus is saying in John 15:8 that the evidence of our connection to the vine is our fruit.

The evidence of our genuine discipleship is the production of other disciples.

This evidence, like building a garden, takes time. The amount of time varies from person to person. But like Thanos from the Marvel

Avenger movies, it is inevitable. As we know a tree by the fruit it produces, so we know a person by the people they produce.

As we discussed in the last chapter, discipleship is natural to us. CrossFit people produce more CrossFit people. Marvel movie fans produce more Marvel movie fans. Jesus followers produce more Jesus followers.

So, let me ask you, do you have evidence of your discipleship? If someone observed your life, would they see you actively seeking to produce other followers of Jesus? Would they be able to read your social media pages and find evidence of your genuine desire to see people follow Jesus?

Making disciples can be just as frustrating as gardening. Especially, when you have a passion, but are unsure why things don't take root and produce fruit.

In this chapter, I hope to help remove that frustration and confusion. I believe that disciple-making is simply helping another person know and become more like Jesus. That is it! It doesn't have to be complicated. Whether you are discipling your children, a friend, co-worker, neighbor, relative, or complete and utter stranger, it is extremely simple. Help them know and follow Jesus.

We disciple someone as we help them know and follow Jesus. The discipleship process we see in scripture is *intentional interactive instruction.*

Intentional

Is it possible to unintentionally disciple someone? Absolutely! As people interact with Christians in the office, clubs, neighborhood hangouts, sports team, gym, and other various activities, they will observe and learn biblical truth. God may even use these unintentional interactions to start that person's genuine conversion or assist in the growth of another believer. However, discipleship is primarily a personal intentional decision.

Look at how Jesus calls the twelve disciples. In Matthew 4:19, He came to Peter and Andrew and said: "follow me and I will make you fishers of men." James and John appear to have just been called out of the boat they were working in with their father (v.21). Levi was ripping people off, like most tax collectors, when Jesus called him (Luke 5:27-29). In Galilee, Jesus found Philip and called him. Then Philip ran and got Nathanael, who needed a little convincing (John 1:43-51). The others seem to have been selected out of the larger group that was following Jesus early on (Luke 6:12-15).

The point is Jesus intentionally chose to interact and instruct these men. As Jesus says in John 15:16, "You did not choose me, but I chose you and appointed you that you should go and bear fruit and that your fruit should abide."

*Disciple-making starts with an **intentional** decision to spend time with a person.*

Time is one of our most coveted commodities. We love our time. We want more time. Every instance we decide to do something, we are trading time for something. Time, perhaps even more than money, is a powerful indicator of what we value.

Here is an exercise. Open a separate note file on your phone. Record in large chunks what you spend your time on for one whole week. Have the categories as specific, or broad as you like, so long as they accurately account for how you spent your time. Analyze the data. Separate the data into free time (i.e. entertainment) and forced time (i.e. work). Look at your free time. My assumption is you will see clearly what you value.

Disciple making requires sacrificing time. But this intentional decision to help someone know and follow Jesus is not meant to be one-sided. Discipleship is extremely interactive.

Interactive

The best professor I ever had went on a run with me. I remember it clearly. We had just finished a four-hour discussion block on soteriology and were breaking for the evening. My mind was fried. As with any class on soteriology, I had a couple of questions. I went up to ask them privately to the professor after class was dismissed. His response surprised me.

"Jared, do you like to run?" he said, completely sidelining my theological problematic questions.

The next morning, we went on a six-mile run. We went back and forth from rich theological discussion to our common interest in mountaineering. Afterward, we grabbed something to drink and chatted a little longer before cleaning up for class. I have never forgotten that day. My professor chose to not only sacrifice his time, but to interact with me.

The last chapter we talked about our created desire for intimate relational community. Discipleship satisfies an aspect of that created desire, through intentional interaction with each other to glorify and worship God.

When Jesus called the disciples, he didn't spend much time lecturing them, He lived with them. He didn't seek to be served by them, He served them (Mark 10:45). He ate with them, traveled with them, went to parties with them, and probably laughed a lot with them.

Disciple-making is intentionally allowing and seeking life

168

interaction with someone. Let someone see the way you sacrifice for Jesus. Not so they can praise you, but so that they can learn from you. Be open about your struggles with obedience. Show them how to demonstrate love to others. Be a living example of the truth of Jesus Christ and let someone interact with your life.

My professor did nothing groundbreaking. He invited me to interact with him on a run. And I will never forget it. But he didn't just talk to me about life, he talked with me about truth. Intentional interaction, without truth filled instruction, falls short of discipleship.

Instruction

Disciple-making occurs as we intentionally interact and instruct someone to know and follow Jesus. Notice, this is the process of disciple-making. This is not a formula to make disciples. Those two things are significantly different. Instruction on God's truth provides an opportunity to respond.

We can "Do Life" with hundreds of people, and never disciple anyone. Intentional time and interaction don't allow a person to encounter God's truth. Christianity today has shifted to a dangerous position. We are so scared to offend someone, that we resort to saying absolutely nothing definitive. We nod our heads, show empathy, and just hope people encounter truth through a sermon, book, blog, or Facebook post. Rather, what we need, both Christian to Christian and Christian to non-Christian, is a continual reminder and focus upon truth.

We have talked about John 6 earlier in the book. In John 6 something odd happens. Actually, a lot of odd things happen, but one is wild. After Jesus walks on water, makes a ton of bread from a few loafs, He says something that causes everyone to pause. In John 6:35, He says, "I am the bread of life, whoever comes to me shall not hunger; and whoever believes in me shall never thirst." But He didn't stop there, He continues in verse 53 "truly, truly, I say to you, unless you eat the flesh of the Son of Man and drink his blood, you have no life in you." Suddenly, people start asking a lot of questions. Then the crowd could not take His words anymore.

John 6:66 "After this many of his disciples turned back and no longer walked with him."

Notice the word "disciples" used here. These were followers of Jesus! And they walked away. Why? Because they encountered hard instruction that they could not accept. Which, according to verse 64, revealed they never were *true* disciples.

The word of God is living and active. A person's salvation and acceptance of truth is in God's sovereign hands and is according to His grace. But in the words of Paul, "How then will they call on him in whom they have not believed? And how are they to believe in him of whom they have never heard? And how are they to hear without someone preaching? (Romans 10:14).

The process of disciple-making occurs as a person encounters Jesus through another person. This happens as we intentionally interact and instruct each other in God's truth to know and follow Jesus.

Failed Discipleship

I was frustrated. I was heartbroken. Tears flowed uncontrollably down my face as I knelt there on the cold concrete floor of the church's basement. After three years of consistent prayer, teaching, small groups, meetings, opening my home, and youth retreats one student broke me.

He looked into my eyes with a cold and bitter gaze. After a pause, he said, "I don't care. I don't believe in God. I don't want

Him."

I had no response.

All the words had been spoken. All the time was given. He knew the truth, chose to reject it, and I couldn't shake the feeling as though I had failed.

It is unfortunately common to feel as though we are failing at discipleship.

Maybe you have spent years investing and praying for someone to fully embrace Jesus, but they choose to reject Him. Or they came to faith, continued for a while, and then gradually or suddenly fell away. The feeling of personal failure can be overwhelming. Especially if that person is a son or daughter.

I want to encourage us both with the following reality:

There is no such thing as failed discipleship.

When we faithfully give intentional interaction and instruction focused on following Jesus, the Spirit is responsible for the results. John 3:8, "The wind blows where it wishes, and you hear its sound, but you do not know where it comes from or where it goes. So it is with everyone who is born of the Spirit." The Holy Spirit is responsible for the results in disciple making. Whether it be leading an unbeliever to surrendering to Christ, or helping another brother or sister in Christ grow in their following of Jesus. We are only called to be faithful. To not quit when it is hard. God will handle the results of our efforts; our responsibility is to be obedient.

This doesn't mean we can have a "half-hearted" approach in discipleship. No one should ever say of someone who chooses to reject discipleship of Jesus, "Well, they must not have been called by the Spirit." We should strive for them with maximal effort, while completely relying upon God's grace to see that person believe and follow Jesus.

We are called to continue to sacrifice, obey, love, and disciple others for the sake of the glory of Jesus Christ. Regardless of the results.

I had just finished my first deployment. My family and I wanted to visit the church that had blessed us, and continues to bless us deeply, and sent us off to join the military. Never have we encountered a body of believers that so loved and cared for each other as those in this church. We have many incredible friendships and relationships that we are consistently humbled by. We were eager to go back, see, and visit with all these wonderful people.

When we arrived, we were greeted by multiple friends in the church. Amidst the hugs, smiles, and laughing, a name kept coming up. In respect for his actual name, we will call him Adam.

"Did you hear about Adam?!" people would ask.

"Amazing what has happened in the life of Adam." Others would exclaim.

Admittedly, I was suspect and somewhat in disbelief when I heard that Adam had professed faith in Jesus and was baptized. Was this truly the same student who four years previously had put me on my knees in tears on the youth room floor? Was he really following Jesus? Sadly, I was genuinely doubtful. Until I saw him.

He changed. Obviously, his physique had changed, but his presence was different. He smiled. He spoke with a calm confidence and the clear presence of conviction. I was amazed. Four years later and I was on the verge of breaking into tears again. The Spirit had moved in his heart.

We never know what God is doing in the "Adams" of our lives. I would love to tell you that every single-story ends as it did with Adam. Unfortunately, I could describe over a dozen other stories where the individual is still wandering from the Lord.

There is no such thing as failed discipleship when we faithfully proclaim the truth of Jesus.

We are called to faithfully and truthfully walk alongside others for the glory of Jesus. The results are His. We remain faithful, intentionally interacting and instructing others in His truth for His glory.

Summary

A true disciple will disciple others. The evidence of our faith should be seen in the lives of those we interact with. The results are His. We must remain faithful. Disciple-making might sound a lot like living as a Christian. That's because it is. Discipleship is the manifestation of a truly transformed born again Christian.

What does this all look like then in daily life? What does it look like to be discipled according to Jesus' standard of discipleship? What does it look like to disciple according to Jesus' standard of discipleship? How does S.O.L.D., the marks of a true disciple, affect the way I live my life as a follower of Christ?

This is the content of the last chapter.

Chapter 11:
S.O.L.D Out

A True Disciple will be S.O.L.D. out for Jesus

"When Christ calls a man, he bids him come and die."
— Dietrich Bonhoeffer

To be a disciple is to die. Your former self perishes and a new being is born. I have mentioned this verse several times, in Galatians 2:20, Paul said it this way, "I have been crucified with Christ. It is no longer I who live, but Christ who lives in me. And the life I now live in the flesh I live by faith in the Son of God, who loved me and gave himself for me." This is true of all disciples of Jesus. A disciple's life is no longer their own, they are to be a S.O.L.D. out slave of Jesus Christ.

We cannot afford to take discipleship lightly. The risk and danger are too high.

If the commands and expectations of a disciple is synonymous to a born-again Christian, then a significant portion of the professing Christian community is living in disobedience to God.

One of the most terrifying passages in scripture is Matthew 7:21-23.

"Not everyone who says to me, 'Lord, Lord,' will enter the kingdom of heaven, but the *one who does the will of my Father who is in heaven.* [22] On that day many will say to me, 'Lord, Lord, did we not prophesy in your name, and cast out demons in your name, and do many mighty works in your name?' [23] And then will I declare to them, 'I never knew you; depart from me, you workers of lawlessness.'"

The evidence of true belief is surrender to God's will. If there is no surrender to the will of God, then there is no genuine faith. The most terrifying thing in the world is to live thinking and believing you are saved, only to be cast out upon the day of accountability. Every professing Christian must repeatedly examine their life according to the explicit evidences Jesus says will be present in every true disciples' life.

In Matt 7:21-23, those who were cast out had done mighty works in the name of Jesus. The error of those cast out was that they took confidence in their own works rather than the work of Jesus. Modern Christianity has turned into an organization measured with numbers, budgets, and social works. Churches solidify and evaluate their faithfulness and effectiveness by the sound of their band, the raising of hands and closing of eyes, the amount in the offering, the number in the auditorium, and the size of the baptism service. Parents confirm their godliness by other people's perceptions and praise of their children. Singles take confidence in their fidelity by comparing themselves to the conduct of their peers. All the while, God is calling out, "I do not know you!"

Robert Robinson was a pastor, theologian, and musician who lived in the mid to late 1700's.[xliv] He wrote the hymn *Come Thou Fount* when he was twenty-two years old. At this relatively young and influential age, he recognized what Christians continue to affirm, we need God's grace daily to sustain and guide us. His third verse was originally written this way:

Oh, to grace how great a debtor

175

Daily I'm constrained to be!
Let that grace now, like a fetter,
Bind my yielded heart to Thee.
Let me know Thee in Thy fullness;
Guide me by Thy mighty hand,
Till, transformed, in Thine own image
In Thy presence I shall stand.

Every day is a complete trust and reliance upon the grace of God. Robinson uses the term "fetter", which means chain or shackle, to describe how grace is to bind a disciple's heart to Jesus. To be a disciple is to be a slave of Jesus, to know Him in His fulness. To say with Paul, "But whatever gain I had, I counted as loss for the sake of Christ. [8] Indeed, I count everything as loss because of the surpassing worth of knowing Christ Jesus my Lord. For His sake I have suffered the loss of all things and count them as rubbish, in order that I may gain Christ" (Phil. 3:7-8). The disciple continues to be bound by grace to Jesus until that final day when their joy is complete, and they stand in His presence.

David Platt, Pastor-Teacher at McLean Bible Church, wrote about Jesus' unique call in a small book titled *What did Jesus mean when he said Follow Me?* He wrote in the introduction:

"Ultimately the call to follow Jesus is a call to die —to die to ourselves and to die to the things of this world. But at the same time, it is a call to live —to experience unbridled joy as we follow Jesus wherever he leads in this world."[xlv]

To be a disciple is to die to yourself and to live to Christ. This is a daily endeavor. As Robinson wrote, "daily I'm constrained to be!" So, what does the S.O.L.D. out disciple look like daily?

A S.O.L.D. out disciple daily seeks to rely on God's grace and surrender to His will.

I want to clarify, this does not mean we are daily questioning and seeking proof of salvation. Disciples live with confidence in the finished work of Jesus Christ. That they are sealed by the indwelling of the Holy Spirit. Nothing can snatch them out of the powerful protective hand of God. However, a true disciple will daily seek God's grace in order to surrender to His commands and seek to accomplish His plan. To do this, personal and community accountability is wise and encouraged.

We have already studied on how Jesus' primary means for discipleship is intentional interactive instruction. In our technological world, we have access to the best sermons, lectures, books, articles, podcasts, blogs, and other resources in our pocket. You can download more literary works on your phone now in a single day, than most people saw in their lifetimes 200 years ago. While these resources are excellent and should be utilized, they are not a substitute for personal relational discipleship.

There are multiple practical ways to seek our intentional interactive instruction to grow as a disciple of Jesus. God has not limited discipleship to certain numbered steps, spiritual disciplines, or methods to rely on His grace and surrender to His will. However, the marks that come out of genuine disciples will be the same, regardless of the procedure.

Significant works have been written describing how to conduct one on one, small group, home group, teams, and organic discipleship relationships. While there are excellent principles we can learn from these methodologies, we cannot miss the core understanding that discipleship is about Jesus and His kingdom, not about our mentor/discipler and a particular church's organizational kingdom.

With that in mind, I want to offer what several practical suggestions that other authors have already provided on how to go about discipleship. The following are a few that either I have used personally, or that have come highly recommended by men who have discipled me.

TEAMS

The discipleship method suggested by Randy Pope, in the book Insourcing, is the idea of Journey Groups and focusing on T.E.A.M.S. for reproducible discipleship.[xlvi]

Randy suggests this is the way to develop, mature, and equip disciples of Jesus Christ. In his book, he devotes a chapter to what the end product of a person should look like, once they have gone through his model.

Again, Randy does specify that disciple and Christian are synonymous. However, his practical method of journey groups offers a simple reproducible model to conduct intentional, interactive, instructional discipleship. Each time these groups come together to help each other follow Jesus, they are to walk through T.E.A.M.S. in order to ensure they spend their time intentionally.

Truth: what God has revealed for his people to know, understand and obey.

Equipping: messaging God's truth into life so that it becomes understandable and usable.

Accountability: asking the hard questions to encourage living fully for Christ.

Mission: engaging with the lost world in order to impart the gospel through word and deed.

Supplication: engaging in conversation with God to express dependence on Him.

This acronym provides a helpful guideline to ensure every time you meet with someone or a group, you are intentional with your time. In the appendix, I offer a 16-week S.O.L.D. study suggestion. Randy's T.E.A.M.S. can easily be incorporated into this study to provide additional organization and consistent flow to the meetings. If you are going to engage in small groups as your primary means for discipling and being discipled, then I highly recommend having some sort of organization for each meeting to ensure your time is spent intentionally.

Discipleship Wheel

Jim Putman, in his book Real-life Discipleship,[xlvii] defines a disciple as a person who is following Christ, being changed by Christ, and doing the mission of Christ. This involves the head, hands, and heart to be surrendered to Jesus. His practical method is focused on equipping leaders to discern the spiritual maturity of those they are discipling. This discernment will allow them to be able to accurately assess what that person needs in that specific season of their faith. He believes the discipleship process is conducted in two parts.

The first is God changing their heart through His Spirit. The second is God using us to sharpen and grow each other to become more like His Son through *Intentional Relationships.*

By *Intentional,* he means it is the job and privilege of every Christian to be a disciple of Jesus and the job of every church to make disciples. Therefore, we are to be actively seeking those whom God has been calling to become His disciples and walk them through into spiritual maturity.

By *Relational*, he means this process is done through integrated relationships and life together. Putman says this involved real teaching, shepherding, transparency and at the core authentic love, while being equally involved in each other's lives. In order to do intentional relational discipleship, the leader of these groups must discern where each person is at, on what Randy calls, the Spiritual wheel and its 5 stages.

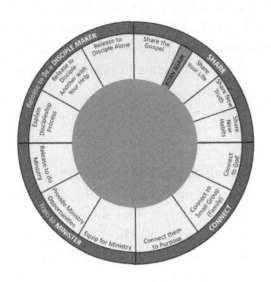

(Fig. 1 – Discipleship Wheel)[xlviii]

Stage 1 involves Share: This is where a leader will discern either spiritual deadness, or infancy of a person and thus share with that person the core basics of the Gospel and Christianity.

Stage 2 involves Connect: If the leader discerns the person to be a Spiritual child, they will seek to connect biblical truths to the heart, as well as connect that person with a small group, church, para church ministry, ect.

Stage 3 involves Minister: If the leader discerns a person to be a spiritual young adult, they will equip that person to minister. Often spiritual young adults can have all the head knowledge and heart however fail in the area of serving others. On this point I disagree with Putman. Jesus calls us from the beginning of our discipleship to serve as He has served. He doesn't tell us to wait and then start serving others. He knows that we learn significantly faster, and in greater detail, as we are actively obeying and serving Him.

Stage 4 involves releasing to disciple: This happens when a leader determines a person is now ready to be a spiritual parent. The leader might take this person under their wing to be a co-discipler for a few months and then release to go disciple.

While I admittedly disagree with several aspects of Putman's wheel, it does provide practical overall guidance for disciple-makers when thinking through the lifespan of their intentional, interactive, and instructional relationship.

Multiply

I have personally gone through Francis Chan's book, *Multiply*,[xlix] with over twenty men in one on one discipleship relationships. Of the multiple practical discipleship resources available, I have found it to be among the best. Francis Chan's book is the method itself. It is meant to be a discipleship tool, that two or more people walk through together, for intentional interactive instruction. The main sections of the book are as follows:

Part I: Living as a Disciplemaker
Part II: Living as the Church
Part III: How to study the Bible
Part IV: Understanding the OT
Part V: Understanding the NT
Part VI: Where do I go from Here?

For every section there are multiple chapters, and in each chapter, there is a link to a video blog from Francis Chan and David Platt with further discussion information. This could be an excellent supplemental study guide, that provides a specific set timeline, and is organized neatly to work through the material. This tool gives freedom to the discipler to venture where they decide. The concepts within S.O.L.D. integrate neatly into the weekly discussions outlined in Multiply.

Three Daily Pursuits

I hope one of these models or another one assists you and others in growing as a disciple of Jesus. I have found that different models work well in different contexts, so long as the definition of a disciple is clear, and the instruction is sound.

I live an extremely diverse and ever-changing life. The first thing I was told before coming into the military is get comfortable being uncomfortable. Things change every day. My schedule is rarely the same from one week to the next. Therefore, what has helped me in my personal discipleship journey, and what I hope can help you, is to remember three daily pursuits: Be Discipled; Make Disciples; Seek to Serve. If you can think about these three things every day, they will hold you personally accountable to walk in the way of the Master.

Be Discipled

Seek intentional, interactive, and instructional discipleship with a person of the same gender, who is preferably one or more seasons of life older than you, for a specific amount of time.

Intentionally ask this person to enter a discipleship relationship. This is not "doing life" together. Nor is this asking for a "mentor" to give practical life help. This relationship should be hyper focused on being a follower of Jesus Christ. While one person can disciple multiple people in an intentional setting, I recommend not having any more than three people to one discipler. Set up specific times to meet either face to face or to talk on the phone. Have a specific purpose for every meeting. Walk through each mark of a disciple and honestly assess how this aspect is going in your life. Take time to systematically study scripture, theological concepts, church history, and other topics. However, never let a study end with theory. Actively seek to integrate your discussion into what God might be calling you to sacrifice or obey, or what person to love or disciple.

Interact together with life enjoyments and struggles. Ask this person for the ability to call if there is a difficult decision, need specific prayer, or confess sin. Be willing to bring this person into your home so that they can observe how you interact with your spouse, children, or those you live with. Invite them to visit your work so that they can have a context to understand your occupation and those you interact with weekly. Be willing to be vulnerable, let this person into painful memories and the unpleasant aspects of your life.

Instruction will only be as beneficial as you make it. If you do not study the agreed upon material, take time for introspection, and honestly evaluate S.O.L.D. in your life, then the benefits of your intentional interaction will be stifled. Whenever you meet, choose one of the four marks to focus on. Specifically, look at sections of scripture or theological concepts that deal with that one mark. Then bridge the gap from theory to practice, thinking through how that concept applies to your walk with Jesus.

When you seek out this relationship, ask for a specific agreed upon schedule and time frame. It is preferable to meet at least once every week. If that is too difficult with schedules, try to meet biweekly face to face and then have a scheduled phone call on the off weeks. Additionally, agree on a specific time frame. It may be that this person will be your discipler for all your life, but circumstances will make this unlikely. Having a specific set amount of time provides both parties with the ability to intentionally plan out an instructional calendar. Having an end point also allows for honest reflection, if the relationship was beneficial and should continue, or if one party wishes the relationship to cease in its current capacity.

At first, I recommend a 16-week commitment. This is enough time to study and discuss the four marks of genuine discipleship and allows for enough time to accurately assess the effect of the relationship. Once this time has expired, reevaluate and decide a duration for the next period of time, and if you need to increase or decrease the frequency of meetings.

There are going to be seasons of life where you do not have this sort of relationship. You may have just moved states, changed churches, or you have traveled to the mission's field and it is just you for a season. However, all of us should actively seek to shorten these seasons to the degree that is possible with our own circumstance.

While intentional meetings might be taking place weekly, the effect of seeking to be discipled happens daily. Morning devotions, studying the instructional material, daily prayer, exercising the applications of scripture, memorizing scripture, and writing things down to discuss at the next meeting happen every day. This activity helps form gospel lenses that change how the disciple sees daily events.

The responsibility is upon every disciple of Jesus to seek out personal accountability by humbly asking another saved sinner to help them become more like Jesus. Additionally, it is equally their responsibility to help others become more like Jesus.

Make Disciples

Making disciples for Jesus begins with prayer. You can imagine it might be a little weird to walk up to a person and say, "Hey! I want to disciple you." That might not be received the best. I believe the process of making disciples starts with praying and asking God who he wants you to disciple. As God puts specific people on your heart, begin praying for them intentionally.

Pray for their genuine discipleship of Jesus. Pray that they would seek to sacrifice, obey, love, and disciple others. Pray for their knowledge of sin and grace. Pray for their conscience to be convicted of disobedience and that they would run to repentance. Pray for their relationships, occupation, finances, family, ministry, and future. As you pray for them, seek to serve them in practical ways. Invite them over for dinner, ask them to attend an activity, or suggest they join you in a practical ministry you participate in.

If that person appears to be receptive in the relationship, then ask them if they are being discipled by anyone. Now, depending on the persons spiritual maturity, those might not be the right words. If they are very new to the faith, perhaps it is as simple as asking, "Would you like to start meeting together to study how to be a follower of Jesus?"

If the person agrees, then you simply model what you are already doing with the person discipling you. Seek to intentionally interact and instruct that person on how to be a S.O.L.D. out follower of Jesus.

By seeking to be discipled and praying to disciple, you practically align your mentality daily to the grace and will of God. John 6:40 says, " For this is the will of my Father, that everyone who looks on the Son and believes in him should have eternal life, and I will raise him up on the last day." By focusing on being and making disciples, we set our gaze on Jesus, His work and plan, and humbly submit ourselves to it. When our mindset is how can I sacrifice, obey, love, and disciple today, it creates a heart that seeks to serve.

Seek to Serve

If it wasn't already clear, it should be now. It is all about Jesus. "For even the Son of Man came not to be served but to serve, and to give his life as a ransom for many" (Mark 10:45). If Jesus came to serve and give Himself for others, then naturally the fruition of discipleship is to become like Him and do the same.

My life is not about my reputation, kingdom, legacy, or accomplishments. It is about Jesus. My life is about His reputation, His kingdom, His legacy, and accomplishing His plan. One of the simplest and practical daily ways we can keep ourselves focused on this mission is to serve.

Seek to serve your Family

Ask every day, "how can I serve my family?" The answer to this question will potentially change daily. Some days, it might be cook dinner. Other days, it might be come home from work early. Each day may be different, but if you don't ask the question, you will become distracted with all the other things you "have" to do. We wrongly think we "have" to do X, Y, and Z throughout the day, otherwise we won't be successful or happy. But when success is measured by our discipleship of Jesus, it refocuses what we actually "have" to do.

Seek to serve the Local Church

Ask every day, "how can I serve my Local Church?" You are saved into the church. How are you actively seeking to serve the body of believers in your area? How can you encourage your leadership? What needs are there that you might be uniquely equipped to assist with? Perhaps, the most significant act of service you can do that day is pray for your pastor and elders. Or for the missionaries your church supports.

Seek to serve Co-Workers

Ask every workday, "how can I serve my Co-Workers?" Once you park your car and turn off the engine immediately take three minutes. That is all, three minutes. Ask yourself this question before you look at your phone or open the door, "In what ways can I serve those I work with today?" Pray that God would provide you opportunities to show His love to them through your service.

Seek to serve your Neighborhood

Ask every day, "how can I serve my neighbors?" What can you do to serve those on your street, in your town, or areas within your city? How can you serve just one person today? If you make it that simple, you will be surprised by the results of what God does with the simplest acts of service.

Seek to serve the Unreached

Ask every day, "how can I serve the unreached?" Luke 19:10 says, "For the Son of Man came to seek and to save the lost." Every day, we must align ourselves to Jesus' mission to seek and save the lost. Reaching the unreached seems like a daunting task. Often these are people who speak different languages than us or live in an area far away. But like any race or mountain climb, it begins with a step. Pray for them. Read about unreached people groups. Encourage those already serving them. Ask those people and organizations who you can do to serve. Just one thing every day, will equal 365 things in a year, and 3,650 in ten years.

Summary

David Platt explains the Christian message well when he writes:

"This is the stunning message of Christianity: Jesus died for you so that He might live in you. Jesus doesn't merely improve your old nature; He imparts to you an entirely new nature —one that is completely united with his. Everything that belongs to him becomes yours. His righteousness replaces your unrighteousness. His Spirit fills your spirit. His love becomes your love. His joy becomes your joy. His mind becomes your mind. His desires become your desires. His will becomes your will. His purpose becomes your purpose. His power becomes your power. The Christian life thus becomes nothing less than the outliving of the indwelling Christ. This is the essence of what it means to be a Christian —a follower of Christ."[1]

To be a disciple of Jesus is to die. To surrender your will to His will. To give over your passions to embrace His passion. To rely upon His grace every day to accomplish His will. If you can remember these three daily pursuits, be discipled, make disciples, and seek to serve, you will hold yourself personally accountable and be able to accurately measure your discipleship of Jesus Christ.

SOLD: Marks of a True Disciple

Conclusion

1 Prayer and 4 Sentences

"The cost of following Christ is great, for it costs you everything you are. But the reward of following Christ is greater, for you experience everything he is —both now and forever." -- David Platt

The cost of discipleship is both nothing and everything. Today's Christianity needs to remember the Master's call. As Platt says, the reward is experiencing Jesus now and forever. A disciple is not a higher tier Christian. The standard for discipleship is not optional. To be a Christian is to be a disciple.

What are the marks of evidence then for true discipleship?

A true disciple will sacrifice for Jesus.

A true disciple will obey for Jesus.

A true disciple will love for Jesus.

A true disciple will disciple for Jesus.

When these marks are evidenced, there can be genuine confidence in our true discipleship of Jesus. Not the performance of actions, but marks of faith.

Genuine faith will display all four marks in an individual's life. Perhaps not at first. Perhaps imperfectly. But where there is no eventual evidence of these marks, there is no true discipleship of Jesus.

If you finished this book, then you realize to sacrifice, obey, love, and disciple how Jesus demands is impossible apart from the grace of God. When we embrace His power through the indwelling of the Spirit, we can experience the reality of His demands. Not for our glory or self-righteousness, but for His praise and His glory.

What follows might be for some of you the best part of this entire book. It is a challenge that is meant to encourage and rejuvenate a Christian's heart in being S.O.L.D. out for Jesus. Like a CrossFit workout, this will be difficult and might cause you to spiritually perspire. But the reward significantly outweighs the cost!

I want to encourage you, if you are a genuine believer in Jesus, then you have the mind of Christ! You have been reborn. It is no longer you who live, but Christ who lives in you. The life that you used to live is now rubbish compared to knowing the surpassing worth of Christ Jesus. He is your hope, your king, your God, and your friend!

This is my challenge to you:

1 Prayer and 4 Sentences.

1 Prayer

I challenge you to do something you may have never done before in your life. Spend 1 hour in constant prayer with God's word.

Martin Luther once said, "I have so much to do that I shall spend the first three hours in prayer." I know you have a lot to do. That is why I am challenging you to pray uninterrupted for 1 hour.

When you do this, have your phone on silent, except for an alarm telling you when an hour has expired. Have nothing with you but the word of God and a list of passages to reflect on. Go wherever you can speak audibly without bothering anyone, and somewhere no one will disturb you.

Break up your prayer with roughly 15 minutes on each category of a true disciple. Pray through the passages associated with each aspect of a true disciple below. Ask the Lord to either confirm or convict your heart in each area of your walk with Jesus.

- Sacrifice – Luke 14:25-33

- Obey – John 8:31

- Love – John 13:34-35

- Disciple – John 15:8

Once you have ended your time, take a minute of quiet reflection and then write the following four sentences.

4 Sentences

Like every good Southern Baptist sermon, there are some fill in the blanks at the end. I want you to do what you already know in your heart you need to. Write down in these blank spaces, or another forum of your choice, whatever God most impressed upon your heart during that hour of prayer. Do not write something to write something. If there is genuinely no impression from the Lord in a category, then skip over it, or write down what you are already working on. These can be as simple or complex as you like.

1. I am called to Sacrifice _____
   _____.

2. I am called to Obey _____
   _____.

3. I am called to Love _____
   _____.

4. I am called to Disciple _____
   _____.

Once done, take a picture or make a copy and give it to the person God is using to disciple you. Ask them to prayerfully consider intentionally interacting with you for encouragement, accountability, and instruction in these four areas, for a specific amount of time. It could be a week, month, or year. Pick a time that is manageable and realistic for both of you.

Once the agreed-upon time is completed, think through what the Lord did in your life in each category. Praise Him for His work and ask His strength for what still needs more progress.

There is a phrase in the military, "rinse and repeat." It means clean yourself and your gear, take a breath, and get ready to do it again. At a minimum, I recommend doing this process once a year to help provide continual course corrections and ensure you are not taking your salvation in Christ for granted.

Turn this exercise into a full day retreat between just you and God if you have the means. Allow His truth to encompass every aspect of your life. For discipleship requires nothing less than complete and total surrender, but the reward is unimaginable and unquantifiable joy in Jesus.

May the grace of God empower you to live S.O.L.D. out for Jesus Christ!

SOLD: Marks of a True Disciple

Appendix A:

Example 16-week S.O.L.D. Study

This outline was originally intended for Youth Group leaders and their discipleship of the Youth Group's Student Leaders. However, it can be adapted and changed to fit any other particular discipleship context.

Outline:

Week 1: A True Disciple will Sacrifice:

- Explain how a True Disciple is = S.O.L.D. out Follower of Christ
- Memory verse: Luke 14:33
- Purpose: Show how a true disciple will seek to sacrifice for Christ
- Discussion questions:
  - o How does the Gospel compel us to Sacrifice?
  - o What does the life of a person who sacrifices look like?
  - o What are things in your life are you currently sacrificing?
- Optional: Set one sacrificial goal for the next 15 weeks.

Week 2: A True Disciple will Obey:

- Memory verse: John 8:31-32

- Purpose: Show how a true disciple will seek to obey Christ
- Discussion questions:
  - How does the Gospel compel us to Obey? (Look at 1 John 4:17-19)
  - What does the life of a person who obeys look like?
  - How do you know what to obey?
- Optional: Set one obedience goal for the next 14 weeks.

Week 3: A True Disciple will Love:

- Memory verse: John 13:34
- Purpose: Show how a true disciple will seek to Love others for Christ
- Discussion questions:
  - How does the Gospel compel us to Love? (Look at John 14:15)
  - What does the life of a person who loves look like?
  - What does it mean to love someone?
  - What does Christ expect our love will look like?
- Optional: Set one love goal for the next 13 weeks.

Week 4: A True Disciple will Disciple:

- Memory verse: John 15:8
- Purpose: Show how a true disciple will seek to Disciple others for Christ
- Discussion questions:
  - How does the Gospel compel us to Disciple? (Look at John 15:8)
  - What does it mean to disciple someone else?
  - What do you expect from me the person who is discipling you?
  - Who do you think God is calling you to disciple?

- Optional: Set one discipleship goal for the next 12 weeks.

Weeks 5-7: What does it look like for me to Sacrifice

- Select a memory verse for each week or Key study passage.
- Select a purpose for each meeting that you will cover _____ with regard to sacrifice.
- Create a few discussion questions to help guide the conversation
- At Week 5 have a study written up and a goal to keep in-between the next 3 meetings that is measurable and realistic to practical sacrifice for Christ.

Weeks 8-10: What does it look like for me to Obey

- Select a memory verse for each week or Key study passage.
- Select a purpose for each meeting that you will cover _____ with regard to Obey.
- Create a few discussion questions to help guide the conversation.
- At Week 8 have a study written up and a goal to keep in-between the next 3 meetings that is measurable and realistic to practically obey Christ. A good one would be to set up a regular reading of the scriptures for the disciple and yourself.

Weeks 11-13: What does it look like for me to Love

- Select a memory verse for each week or Key study passage – Maybe take one meeting and have the disciple study as many passages as possible on love. Then talk through their thoughts from their scripture reading and about having love for one another.

- Select a purpose for each meeting that you will cover _____ with regard to Love.
- Create a few discussion questions to help guide the conversation.
- At Week 11 have a study written up and a goal to keep in-between the next 3 meetings that is measurable and realistic to practically Love others for Christ.

Week 14-16: What does it look like for me to Disciple others

- Select a memory verse for each week or Key study passage.
   o Definitely, take time to look over John 15 and what Jesus says about bearing fruit.
- Select a purpose for each meeting that you will cover _____ with regard to Discipling.
- Create a few discussion questions to help guide the conversation.
- At Week 14 have a study written up and a goal to keep in-between the next 3 meetings that is measurable and realistic to practically Disciple others for Christ.
   o This goal as well might be able to carry on for longer than the 3 weeks.

What this might look like on any specific day: A Short Youth Leader Story

It was almost 5:30pm. Katie was just about to pull into Samantha's driveway when she parked the van just down the street. Grabbing her Bible, she pulled out her page printout that she had every week for her and Samantha's meetings. She looked over her sheet, which was the last part in their three part series on Sacrifice. After looking over the sheet, confident that she had the memory verse down, and where to steer their discussion, Katie put the sheet back into its place in her bible and closed her eyes. Once she had thanked God for the opportunity to disciple one of His children to become more like His son, and asked for wisdom and the words to speak to Samantha, Katie drove down the street and parked in front of Samantha's gorgeous Victorian three story home. Katie had barely stepped out of the van before she heard Samantha's voice from the perfectly trimmed ivy-covered terrace on the second story.

"Katie! Go ahead and come in! The door is unlocked, I will be down in just a second." Shot Samantha while turning to run down the stairs.

It wasn't easy for Katie, the small-town Christian farm girl, to meet and disciple Samantha. Samantha's Dad was a successful Pediatrician who worked in the city and had a booming practice. From the first time that they discussed sacrifice, Katie knew that this was going to be a hard concept for Samantha to grasp.

Taking off her shoes on the marble floor, Katie waited for Samantha. Without any show of elegance, the 15 year old galloped down the spiral stair case and gave Katie a huge hug.

"Katie, I can't wait to tell you what happened today! Ahhh I am so excited! Let's go out to the patio, my Mom made us Zuppa Tuscana, and baked fresh French bread! I want to tell you all about it." Said Samantha while pulling Katie through the living room out to the magnificent backyard patio. They sat down and Samantha not being able to contain herself began to relay to Katie what had happened that day.

"Okay so you know Micah? I have mentioned him like a couple of times. Definitely the most gorgeous man at school. Well today, I could kind of see him hanging out by my locker. I totally pretended not to notice him, but of course, I like did..."

Katie was already eyeing her soup that was cooling down, her unopened bible and the clock over the grill that kept clicking away.

"...anyways, out of the corner of my eye I saw him start to come over, walking right toward me! So, he came over... Oh my gosh I can't believe it still... he said 'hey' and already I was getting so nervous. We talked about like nothing for 3 minutes, and then all the sudden he asked me if I wanted to go to the movies Friday! AHHH I am so excited!" Said Samantha while still shaking.

Katie smiled and laughed with Samantha, but inwardly she was fighting with herself. Her Bible was still on the table unopened. Katie debated ending that conversation there with a "that's great" and getting into their study, or if she should continue letting Samantha go on about this boy. Just then she remembered that Christ walked with the disciples for 3 years in everyday life and probably entertained quite a few seemingly spiritually unimportant conversations that were important to the disciples. So, Katie entertained Samantha and kept the questions coming.

"No way! Okay so show me a picture!" Samantha pulled up his Facebook and they creeped his page and laughed over some of his pics. They watched a highlight video from last week's football game, Samantha clearly proud of her teen romance interest.

Then Katie remembered the goal that her and Samantha set at their first meeting with regards to sacrifice. Being a somewhat new believer, Samantha wanted to stop listening to non-Christian music and separate herself for a time from hanging out with non-Christian people one on one, because she realized she wasn't strong enough in her faith to influence them, but rather they were influencing her. So, Katie asked,

"So, where does Micah go to church?" Samantha seemed a little thrown off by her questions.

"Ah not sure, why?" Said Samantha, with a little excitement fading.

"Well I am just curious what his beliefs are. An easy way to tell is by what sort of church he goes to." Said Katie like a matter of fact.

"I get that, but I don't really know." Responded Samantha, now seeming awkwardly quiet.

"Okay, well from talking with him, or what you know of him what do you think he believes?" Asked Katie, now a little worried.

"I don't know" responded Samantha, this time very short.

"Samantha, I hope you don't mind me asking, but is Micah a professing Christian?" Katie asked straight up.

Samantha paused. She didn't look at Katie. She then said under her breath;

"No, he isn't."

At this point the Zuppa Tuscana wasn't the only thing that was cold. Katie could see that Samantha knew where she was going.

"I see. Do you remember three weeks ago when we first started talking about sacrifice?" Asked Katie.

"Yes" said Samanatha.

"Well after our discussion of how Christ has sacrificed for us by giving himself, he also calls us to give ourselves for him, I asked you if there was anything that you thought was a struggle for you that needed to be sacrificed for Christ. You immediately responded with non-Christian music and non-Christian friends. Would this date be going against what you feel God is calling you to sacrifice?" Asked Katie as gently as she could.

Samantha had no response. She was silent and completely shut down.

Katie tried again, "I am not saying that this is inherently wrong or a sin to go on the date, but I just want to question you because you told me that you felt these two areas were distracting you from growing in Christ. What do you think?"

Samantha this time only muttered. "I don't know."

The evening was cut short by the awkward silence. They finished their cold soup with nothing more than a few off-hand comments and half-hearted smiles. A few minutes later Samantha said she had a lot of homework so maybe they could reschedule to another time for the study. But Samantha offered no date to meet up. Katie put her shoes on and got into her van, and looked at her unopened bible and just prayed that what she had said was right and that God would work in Samantha's heart. She backed up and started the drive home.

Discipleship Doesn't Always Go the Way we Imagine

Sometimes saying what you believe needs to be said won't end well immediately. Sometimes you will meet, and your Bible will not even be opened. Life is difficult and both discipling and being discipled can be a painful process because we are dealing with sin. Sanctification happens over time. That is why we love the person like crazy and trust in God to work through His truth and make us and other S.O.L.D. out disciples for Him.

ABOUT THE AUTHOR

Jared M Price (B.A., Moody Bible Institute; M.A., Southern Baptist Theological Seminary) served as a young adults and youth pastor for 4 years at Cornerstone Bible Church in Westfield, Indiana. After significant prayer, confirmation from his wife Janelle, and the blessing of the elders of Cornerstone, he decided to join the United States Navy to serve as an Officer. Him and his wife Janelle, and their three daughters, Maggie, Audrey, and Emma, live in San Diego, California.

Jared is passionate about serving Jesus in every aspect of his life. In addition to military service, Jared started Storm Packs LLC with his brother Nathan, in order to help provide practical quality emergency equipment to prepare people for natural disasters. Storm Packs LLC assists with natural disaster relief acts in the United States and looks toward global assistance in the future.

You can find out more about Jared at www.jaredmprice.com or contact him at marksofadisciple@gmail.com

i Wilkins, M. J. (1992). *Following the master: discipleship in the steps of Jesus* (Part I: Chapter 2). Michigan: Zondervan Publishing House.

ii Pope, R., & Murray, K. (2013). *Insourcing: bringing discipleship back to the local church.* Grand Rapids, MI: Zondervan.

iii Putman, J. (2014). *Real-life discipleship building churches that make disciples.* United States: The Navigators.

iv Louw, J. P., & Nida, E. A. (1996). *Greek-English lexicon of the New Testament: based on semantic domains* (electronic ed. of the 2nd edition., Vol. 1, p. 470). New York: United Bible Societies.

v For additional information on the Greco-Roman understanding of discipleship see Wilkins, M. J. (1992). *Following the master: discipleship in the steps of Jesus* (Part II: Chapter 4). Michigan: Zondervan Publishing House.

vi Ibid. Part II: Chapter 4. See this chapter for further information on the term "disciple" in the Greco-Romans world.

vii Ibid. Part II: Chapter 5.

viii Ibid. Part III: Chapter 6.

ix Gallaty, R., & Collins, R. (2013). *Growing up: how to be a disciple who makes disciples.* Bloomington, IN: CrossBooks Pub.

x For additional practical suggestions on methods and practices see: McCallum, D., Lowery, J., McCallum, D., & Lowery, J. (2012). *Organic discipleship: mentoring others into spiritual maturity and leadership.* Columbus, OH: New Paradigm.

xi Dodson has excellent insight in shaping our worldview to be framed in the fundamentals of Christianity. I do not believe his understanding of discipleship to be wrong, just simply not specific enough. For further research and study see: Dodson, J. K. (2012). *Gospel-centered discipleship.* Wheaton, IL: Crossway.

[xii] Dodson's definition is not wrong, just simply incomplete. The church needs to understand that the expectations placed upon disciples are the same for anyone who calls themselves a Christian. If not, people will wrongly assume that the words of Jesus in regard to discipleship, do not apply to them. Ibid.

[xiii] I concur with Wilkens definitions and believe they are the most biblically faithful and understandably succinct. Wilkins, M. J. (1992).

[xiv] Here is my fundamental disagreement with Gallaty. A disciple cannot be considered luke warm, for this is the very object of God's wrath in this Revelation passage. To entertain this idea is to provide professing Christians with a false sense of eternal security that could jeopardize their relationship with God. See: Gallaty, Collins (2013).

[xv] Bonhoeffer, D. (2015). *The cost of discipleship.* London: SCM Press.

[xvi] Horton, M. S. (2012). *The gospel-driven life* (p. 26). Grand Rapids, MI: BakerBooks.

[xvii] For further research on Antinomianism and Legalism see: Jones, M. (2013). *Antinomianism: Reformed theologys unwelcome guest?* Phillipsburg, NJ: P & R Pub.

[xviii] Jones attempts to solidify the reality of union to Jesus Christ through the Holy Spirit. For Jones, all the problems that Antinomians raise against Reformed Theology is answered and satisfied in the concept of union to Christ. See: Ibid.

[xix] Louw, J. P., & Nida, E. A. (1996). *Greek-English lexicon of the New Testament: based on semantic domains* (electronic ed. of the 2nd edition., Vol. 1, p. 470). New York: United Bible Societies.

xx Swanson, J. (1997). *Dictionary of Biblical Languages with Semantic Domains : Hebrew (Old Testament)* (electronic ed.). Oak Harbor: Logos Research Systems, Inc.

xxi John Frame's Systematic Theology is an excellent resource on a wide array of Christian beliefs. He provides succinct and understandable definitions with helpful illustrations to grasp the concepts. For further study and research see: Frame, J. M. (2013). *Systematic theology: an introduction to Christian belief*. Phillipsburg, NJ: P&R Publishing.

xxii See Grudem's section on the Atonement: Grudem, W. A., & Thoennes, K. E. (2008). *Systematic theology*. Grand Rapids, MI: Zondervan.

xxiii Trevor Joy's sermons and other excellent biblical resources can be found at: https://www.tvcresources.net/resource-library

xxiv For a short summary on the life and legacy of Bonhoeffer, see: Galli, M., & Olsen, T. (2000). Introduction. In *131 Christians everyone should know* (p. 380). Nashville, TN: Broadman & Holman Publishers.

xxv For an interesting interpretation and perspective on the experiments see: Mcleod, S. (2017, February 5). The Milgram Experiment. Retrieved from https://www.simplypsychology.org/milgram.html

xxvi Hamilton, J. M. (2010). *Gods glory in salvation through judgment: a biblical theology*. Wheaton, Ill: Crossway. Chapter 2.

xxvii Horton, M. S. (2012). *The gospel-driven life* (p. 64). Grand Rapids, MI: BakerBooks.

xxviii Both Calvin and Arminius agreed that before the foundation of the world, God elected true believers in him. However, they came to two drastically different understandings of that predetermined election. For Calvin, the election was specific and irrefutable. For Arminius, it was united with God's foreknowledge, he chose those who he foreknew would choose him. This is an oversimplification, but the specific details of each position is unnecessary to understand obedience is impossible apart from God's grace.

xxix Galli, M., & Olsen, T. (2000). Introduction. In *131 Christians everyone should know* (p. 378). Nashville, TN: Broadman & Holman Publishers.

xxx Edwards, J. (2012). *Treatise concerning religious affections* (p. 1). Place of publication not identified: Rarebooksclub Com.

xxxi Ibid. (p. 6).

xxxii For the overview of Horatio Spafford's life see his Wikipedia article at: Horatio Spafford. (2019, September 18). Retrieved from https://en.wikipedia.org/wiki/Horatio_Spafford

xxxiii Galli, M., & Olsen, T. (2000). Introduction. In *131 Christians everyone should know* (p. 279). Nashville, TN: Broadman & Holman Publishers.

xxxiv For the full message from John Piper go to: https://www.desiringgod.org/messages/love-one-another-for-love-is-of-god

xxxv I recommend that Richard Dawkins book to be read in its entirety. Every Christian should be ready to give a defense for their faith, and an excellent place to start is by examining the arguments of this highly praised atheist in his New York Times best seller. For further study see: Dawkins, R., & Dennett, D. C. (2016). *The God delusion*. London: Black Swan.

xxxvi Hitchens, C. (2017). *God is not great: how religion poisons everything*. London: Atlantic Books.

xxxvii Quell, G., & Stauffer, E. (1964–). ἀγαπάω, ἀγάπη, ἀγαπητός. G. Kittel, G. W. Bromiley, & G. Friedrich (Eds.), *Theological dictionary of the New Testament* (electronic ed., Vol. 1, p. 37). Grand Rapids, MI: Eerdmans.

xxxviii See: https://www.dictionary.com/browse/forgiveness

xxxix To listen to this sermon see the following reference: You Will Never Be Thirsty Again. (2019, September 21). Retrieved from https://www.desiringgod.org/messages/you-will-never-be-thirsty-again

xl Wilson, J. P. (1814). *A body of divinity*. Philadelphia: Woodward.

xli You Will Never Be Thirsty Again. (2019, September 21). Retrieved from https://www.desiringgod.org/messages/you-will-never-be-thirsty-again

xlii To read the full story, I recommend reading through *The End of the Spear*: Saint, S. (2005). *End of the spear*. Wheaton, IL: Tyndale House Publishers.

xliii Swanson, J. (1997). *Dictionary of Biblical Languages with Semantic Domains : Hebrew (Old Testament)* (electronic ed.). Oak Harbor: Logos Research Systems, Inc.

xliv My understanding of Robert Robinson in limited to several articles online. Namely, the following article from Christianity.com served as most of my insight: Did Robert Robinson Wander as He Feared? (2010, April 28). Retrieved from

https://www.christianity.com/church/church-history/timeline/1701-1800/did-robert-robinson-wander-as-he-feared-11630313.html

xlv Platt, D. (2013). *What did Jesus really mean when He said Follow me?* Carol Stream, IL: Tyndale House Publishers.

xlvi Pope, R., & Murray, K. (2013). *Insourcing: bringing discipleship back to the local church.* Grand Rapids, MI: Zondervan.

xlvii Putman, J. (2014). *Real-life discipleship building churches that make disciples.* United States: The Navigators.

xlviii The Process Of Disciple Making – The Discipleship Wheel (Free Resource!). (n.d.). Retrieved from https://jimputman.com/2018/11/10/the-process-of-disciple-making-the-discipleship-wheel-free-resource/

xlix Chan, F., Beuving, M., & Platt, D. (2013). *Multiply: disciples making disciples.* Detroit: Christian Large Print.

l Platt, D. (2013). *What did Jesus really mean when He said Follow me?* Carol Stream, IL: Tyndale House Publishers.

Made in the USA
Middletown, DE
26 February 2022

61868548R00126